Close on the Farm

Survival of the Funniest

Tales of a Free-range Childhood

By Alex R. Weddon

PURE MICHIGAN®
Your trip begins at michigan.org

Volume one, number four

Published by Jones Lake Press
copyright 2013 Alex R.Weddon
first edition, paperback January 2013
fourth printing April 2014
ISBN: 978-0-578-11968-7

All rights reserved. No part of this book shall
be reproduced, stored in retrieval systems, or
transmitted by any means without written permission of the author.

Printed in the United States of America by Edwards
Brothers Malloy, Ann Arbor, Michigan.

**The author in his newspaper office,
circa 2010.**

photo by Alex R. Weddon

Table of Contents

On the cover:
Larry Cobb, on left, holding an apple and
a crow. Loyal dog Bozo and Alex with his
trusty popgun.

Photograph taken in the early 1960s by
Amy Weddon Tomlin

Introduction

These are all true stories. Just ask my twin sister, Amy.

I am a twin, the last birth our dear mother had to endure in creating our family of seven. And on her birthday, as luck would have it. My birth records list me at over eight pounds and Amy weighing a parasitized five pounds. It's amazing she wasn't thrown back, not quite being a keeper.

Amy had an advocate in our older sister Patrice, two years older and wise beyond years to us. Todd was the oldest and then Brad. The two boys ran together unless a hot rod or a cute girl was within two hundred yards.

Dad was a WWII G.I. Bill MD. He was a decorated US Army corpsman and his general practice was recognized for excellence by his peers at the county and state level, US senators and governors. Mom, a masters in education, freelance writer, national award winning author and blessed with a sense of optimism and humor that lends credence to the old saw that a happy mom has happy kids.

We grew up on an eighty acre farm in mid-Michigan during the 1960s and early 70s. My father and mother both had successful careers off the farm as did many of our friends and neighboring farmers. Dad practiced medicine three miles away in a town of under two thousand. Mom spent most of her time on the farm writing national award winning books and articles, keeping track of the five kids, managing the home and preparing daily, nap-inducing hot lunches for Dad.

The United States was in an economic growth spurt, life was good. The only nationwide fear was that of nuclear annihilation by a country halfway around the world.

They asked me if I had a good childhood, my Mom when I was going off to college and forty years later my Dad, shortly before his death just a year after Mom passed away. Mom heard a resounding yes and the list of achievements by my senior yearbook picture proves it. Dad heard a heartfelt yes, I had a wonderful childhood. I considered those formative years as normal, but had to modify that impression after hearing my friends relate stories of their youth. Most didn't have the wide open freedom and almost daily adventures I had.

Dad and I shared a few often told stories in the living room of our 1890s farmhouse during his last days and I was encouraged to write them down. I started a list of youthful anecdotes to share during my daily visit to the dying doctor. The easiest memories to recall were the near death experiences. After that, the NDEs of my siblings. After his funeral I started writing the short stories for The Grass Lake Times, a small, rural weekly newspaper I purchased in 2006.

Acknowledgments

I have to thank my parents first of all. It was Mom's idea to purchase the farm just a quarter mile away from their home in Stockbridge, Michigan. She told Dad it was an ideal place to raise a family and they could move into a bigger house and not leave the best neighbors and friends they ever had.

I also have to thank my brothers and sisters. They all saved me from harm or administered first aid at one time or another. Todd, Brad, Patrice and Amy worked smart and hard and by any measure were quite successful with their education and careers and, of course, in raising their children.

Also, my children; Dane, Randi, Mallory and Alaina and wonderful wife, Colleen. Raising four kids gave us a perspective of life that grows more wondrous everyday.

A special thanks to Mary Hashman and sister Patrice for proof reading and to William Latocki for cover design and creative work.

SPRING

Feral at Four

Parents in our neighborhood of farms and single-family homes felt the land, fresh air and the waters of Michigan made the best place to raise a family during the often turbulent and changing 1960s. The kids of this hardworking generation had lots of open spaces and grew up fearless. The year my twin sister and I were born, Mom and Dad had developed their parenting skills over three youngsters and ten years. By the time Amy and I were upright and running around, they were not overly surprised by our achievements or antics.

As long as we were not up too high, playing with a razor-sharp object or near a life-threatening hazard, we were free to roam. It may have looked like a hands-off approach to childrearing, but with older siblings, protective dogs and observant neighbors, Amy and I fully exploited our free range status mostly unfettered.

Mom worked as a freelance writer at home, managing a number of articles in various stages of development and photographs for various newspapers and magazines. Her new electric typewriter sat nestled on an antique desk in the dining room, surrounded with stacks of yellowing single sheets of blank paper, old newspapers, magazines, notebooks, cassette tapes of interviews and carbon paper. The desk hunkered near a window overlooking the east porch. On cloudless mornings the early sun fell through yellowed plastic shades and flooded her work area and dining room with a cheerful brightness.

Our home's only telephone was a standard issue black plastic rotary dial model, next to her cluttered desk. She spent time on it or typing away or both. To round out her multitasking, she kept track of what was boiling or baking in the kitchen and directed the constant stream of human and animal traffic through the house. TV, radio, washing machine and parakeets added to the increasing chatter in the old farmhouse. Somehow, Mom managed all these sensory inputs and still remained calm. Aside from chain smoking and a constant cup of coffee, she wore the stress well.

Before Amy and I were five years old, certain behavior attributed to the two of us may have contributed to the neighborhood consensus that we were untamed animals. Taken out of context, I feel some of our double teamed adventures may have been misjudged. I maintain that my dear twin and I were normal little kids.

9

Eyewitness claims of Amy and me prancing naked in the yard have circulated in the neighborhood for years. I ask this in response: What mother wouldn't take advantage of a warm spring rain to lather up her toddlers and turn them out in a steady downpour?

And as for biting the fingers of a prominent and unsuspecting member of our township's Historical Society, I will admit that we were under the dinner table as Mom interviewed her, but the alleged accost consisted of merely a series of nibbles. Yes, we were naked again and had just jumped from the table as the two came into the room to sit down.

Afterwards, sources attest that the lady related to society members how nice it was to be interviewed by Mrs. Weddon, though she warned future visitors to keep their hands on the table.

On days when four-year-old Amy and I pretended to be horses, our sister Patrice, who was almost three years older, would oblige us by making a barnyard of the living room. She took good care of us, putting raw oatmeal in a mixing bowl and water in another. For our stable, she draped a blanket between the couch and our living room chairs.

The day of the great stampede, Mom had a guest over for coffee and a few questions.

Mrs. B was a retired teacher and was recalling her classroom days in the one room school house almost two miles away. "Kids were so well mannered back then," she remembered wistfully, no doubt referring to the late 1950s when she taught my two older brothers in her red brick school at the end of the lane.

About this time, Amy and I decided to make a break from the confines of the corral in the living room. We emerged from under the blanket on our hands and knees and started feeding and slurping. This drew the old teacher's attention.

After a whinny or two, Amy reared then bolted on all fours through the dining room, past the white-haired disciplinarian. I galloped close behind her and out the screen door with a slam. The teacher caught her breath and gave a pinched look. Seeing this, Patrice hastened to an exit, claiming she was "going to lasso those runaways that are spooking the chickens." Mom continued taking notes and asking questions. Everything seemed normal to her.

The guest asked how old we were. "I just was wondering how long before they were in school," she explained.

"Elementary or obedience?" our mother joked.

Another contributing factor was registered after an incident during a morning visit by our neighbor and Patrice's friend Ritchie. The pair had been outside in the vegetable garden and were strolling up the hill to our house. Amy and I watched them approach from behind a low strung laundry line, intended to keep us on the east porch. Mom wanted us to get some fresh air and sunshine as she worked but didn't want us to wander off since our older sister wasn't there to watch us.

My resourceful twin suggested we greet them and dared me to direct a stream of you-know-what into the air. As expected of a four-year-old, my aim was less than true. What I gave up in accuracy, I made up in volume. With my limited experience, I failed to adjust for the slight breeze and Ritchie was soon doused with a welcoming arc. For some reason, he was not as entertained as we were. In a less than neighborly mood, he went home to change. Before noon, his mother telephoned Mom and lodged a complaint. Not even in school yet, and Amy and I were earning a reputation.

I wouldn't say Amy and I were difficult to watch, but a long line of baby sitters came and went. To slow turnover, Mom adopted a patient approach to breaking in sitters, gradually extending their duty time with us.

One innocent named Lois chased us through the pasture and back to the sanctuary of the barn only minutes after being left in charge.

The fun started as soon as we heard Mother honk a series of decidedly upbeat good-byes from the station wagon. Taking the toots as a cue, Amy and I scampered out the back door and toward open farmland. Lois was a high school cheerleader, and Mom, like most parents, felt cheerleaders to be hardworking and responsible young ladies. Most importantly to Mom, Lois was in good physical condition. Since our school did not have a girls' track team to draw from, our dear mother felt a cheerleader would stand a decent chance of keeping up with her twins.

Over the pasture gate and down the lane we fled. Our steps quickened when we heard the screen door bang. The ponytailed athlete had burst out the door and was gaining speed. The three of us sprinted along the tractor path, our barking dogs joining the high speed chase. Though Lois was after us, she now had to contend with a pack of dogs barking at her heels.

As the newbie sitter closed on us, we headed in opposite directions and bound away like three foot high gazelles. Running from our older siblings was second nature for us and seemed the natural thing to do with a fresh babysitter.

Deep into the pasture, Amy and I doubled back, extending our lead on the loping blonde. The dogs, familiar with this routine, stopped chasing the now winded and slowing Lois to trot back to the homestead. When we entered the sanctuary of the barn, the two of us vaulted into the hayloft and climbed beyond her reach. A few minutes later, Mom returned from her errands in town to see how the rookie sitter was faring during this short exercise.

Mom found her standing guard with the panting dogs in the large barn door opening, hands on her hips, staring up into the haymow.

"I didn't want to catch them," Lois said. "Just wanted to tire them out."

Mom, in the process of shepherding her capering twins out of the barn toward the house, turned and said breathlessly, "Good luck with that."

Spring Snakes

Spring warming was always welcome after a long winter of drifting cold and brief hours of daylight. A sure sign that March's dark cold was yielding to the inevitable spring of April was seeing a snake. And you knew for sure spring was here when one or two were spotted draped on the basement steps of your home.

The farmhouse where I grew up was built over a Michigan basement that had granite and quartz stone walls and a packed dirt floor. Just outside the foundation was an ancient stone cistern. The tomb-like stone igloo collected rain-water for laundry and other non-drinking uses. Neglected for years, it wasn't completely aban-doned. Being deep enough below ground and frost level, it attracted hundreds of milk snakes to hibernate in tangled balls for the winters.

Warm weather would cause the cistern to percolate snakes over the wall and into my world. The hungry snakes easily scaled down to the floor, or would creep along the foundation, looking for food and warmth. Many would find their way up the stairs, onto the landing where the dog food bag was kept. The food attracted rodents and was at ground level.

The migrating snakes could stop by this buffet as they poked their way toward the daylight coming through the chopped hole in the foundation around the well pipe. This convenient exit was directly below the northern and most used door of the home. Encounters were inevitable.

My mother was spooked by a two-footer as our young family came up the sidewalk one Easter Sunday. I was nine years old and remember my mom being afraid. We watched our father catch and kill the snake with his bare hands. It was the first time I saw blood come from a snake.

One of my daily assignments at that mighty age was to feed the dogs. To access the 40 pound bag of dog chow, I'd have to open the basement door, and that was scary because you never knew what would greet you. I'd carefully open the basement door, on guard for a falling broom, fishing pole or steel ice spud that had been hastily left leaning the wrong way. My eyes would sweep the landing for movement around the foodbag, then I'd stretch an arm around the door jamb and to the light switch on the wall a couple feet down the steps. My eyes would fix onto the dimly lighted top stairs and I'd flick the switch. When spring was in the air, it wasn't unusual to be greeted by milk snakes dripping from the stair steps. The critters didn't move fast or shy from my presence, they would lay still, with heads up, and tongues darting out.

I would carefully check to make sure the dog food bag was closed tightly before I'd open it and then scoop out the chow with a Maxwell house coffee can. I didn't bother with the snakes, I was more than happy to leave them alone.

It seemed to me the bigger the snake, the longer the tongue would wag. I believe they play "'possum" when threatened as I have seen them on many occasion stop moving until left alone. This afforded me the opportunity for a close inspection. Once I overcame the initial jolt of seeing a milk snake, I could see the delicate design and coloration that at first glance looks a lot like a rattlesnake.

Snakes always give me a start. My sisters had a closer relationship with the species and were quite familiar with them. We called the most commonly seen and caught snake a "gardener" snake until somebody looked it up and found it to be "Garter" snake.

When one sister would find a snake, the other would try to find a longer one. They would corner me and show me their latest snake trick such as tying a snake into a knot and watching it untie itself.

The girls were more than generous in sharing such newfound knowledge with me. Did you know that if you hold a snake by the tail and wait until the head is hanging down, by using a stirring motion you can make the letter "C." The reptile's head stays near the center axis, so it spins the slowest, just like a figure skater's head when they spin. My twin Amy was demonstrating this phenomenon to me when my older sister Patrice arrived with a Garter snake of her own. The two of them twirled their snakes and chased me around the dinner table for a few laps before Mom redirected their research outside.

So far, I haven't had the opportunity to use their nuggets of wisdom. However, I can turn on a light switch from ten feet away. In the dark and on one foot I might add.

The north face of the old barn.

A Close Call on the Farm

It is a dangerous business, farming. It is the fifth most deadly occupation in the country. I know of accidental deaths on farms on either side of the eighty acres I grew up on and had my share of close calls, as have most farm kids, just ask one.

One such close call came the day our barn caved in on me, my twin sister and boyhood pal.

Larry Cobb was my neighbor and best friend. We shared a love of hunting and outdoors and life without boundaries as most 13-year-old country boys do.

My twin sister and I were in the old barn counting pigeons when he joined us on the main floor of the barn. It was a broken backed, unpainted timber frame barn built over a stone basement at the turn of the century. The frame was hand hewn oak, shaped 12 inches square and cut to accept other bracing timbers. The roof was made of round cherry wood poles under tin sheeting, the barn's second roof. The animals were sheltered in the basement that had doors facing west into the barnyard, while the rest of the foundation was built into the side of a hill using granite and other fieldstone. The second floor was actually the main floor. Our tractor would pull the hay wagons across part of our backyard, past the silo and into the barn from the east side, which was level with our backyard. The entrance was as large as any castle drawbridge opening and often took on that role as Larry and I would storm into it with our just made wooden swords.

On this day we were up to climbing to the top of the hay loft. Ladders had been built into the barn's wall trusses. Amy, Larry and I climbed up the middle wall of the barn to near the roof and stepped onto the uppermost tier of bales. The summer's harvest of hay stacked almost to the roof in the northern part of the barn. A missing plank near the peak was the main source of light, and a gateway for the bats and pigeons to fly through. Pigeons would blast through the narrow slot, across the hay and roost in the other half of the barn.

We could almost reach the rusty, brown iron track rail that hung just under the peak of the barn and ran the length of the roofline. This rail and a pulley were used to move heavy bales up from the wagons or down to the floor. We didn't use it for that, but the rail was just right to loop a rope over to make a swing. Amy went first. She backed up, lifted her feet and sailed out and back. Larry and I elbowed each other for the next turn as Amy came back and let go just as she was about to reverse direction. She landed and was stock still. A perfect swing out and back.

Since we all had been swinging for years, we had developed a variety of techniques. Swinging back upside down was popular. One handed, catching something, throwing something, sitting on the knot and counting how long before having to let go were some of the ways we had fun swinging for hours.

The air was thick with the aroma of Timothy and alfalfa hay and the tang of horse manure. The barn had seen the passing of many generations of animals and their waste in its basement.

Moisture from these sources rose like an acrid cloud to the ceiling of the basement and permeated the oak beams and the main floor planks. All this caused the ceiling beams of the basement to slowly rot. After so many years, the tonnage of hay above was all they could bear.

When I had my turn, I swung out and just before swinging back, let go and dropped. I fell only a few feet but had enough momentum to tilt the balance and the ancient oak and cherry floor beams thirty feet below gave way.

The haymow cracked open and I slid into the middle of the gaping maw. I felt the rough stems of Timothy scratch my upraised arms and my legs were twisted by bales that seemed to tumble in all directions. I kept my eyes open and fended off bales that came at me. I gathered my feet beneath me and drew my arms down and protected my face. The bales were falling with me and I easily made room for myself and managed to stay what I thought was upright.

I had to avoid the crush of others coming from above. I fell to one side, pushing my airborne body out of the swirling chaos and landed on my back, outside of the cascading bales and fractured wood into the summer dried manure of the basement floor. I rolled, stood up and tried to breathe. Seconds had barely passed.

My hands went to my face to adjust my glasses. I could see! I hadn't lost them! That, and not being killed, a miracle. "Thank you Lord!" I croaked from a dry throat.

I made my way over broken beams and bales to an eroded opening in the barn's stone foundation near the silo on the east side. I scaled up and out and walked into a now unfamiliar barn filled with dust and silence. Tall, vertical rays of corn-yellow afternoon sun slashed between the wood planked barn siding and cleaved through the settling dust.

Looking up I saw Amy and Larry. They were standing with their backs against the barn's west wall and were inching sideways on a narrow horizontal wall support pole to a wooden access ladder fifteen feet away. They were about twenty feet up and intensely focused on getting to that ladder and not falling into the abyss that gobbled up their brother and friend.

Larry grabbed the ladder and reached out his other hand to help Amy. They saw me and were relieved to see me alive. They couldn't stop talking as they came down the ladder and made their way across the broken haystack to where I was standing, surrounded by glinting dust motes and golden blades of sun. "I thought for sure you were a goner," Larry blurted.

"There was no way you were gonna make it with the whole summer's worth of hay bales falling on you," Amy declared. "It looked like the hay mow was eating you."

We looked up to the rope hanging from the rail. It was out of reach now, being too far up and away from a wall.

There would be no more swinging from it - no way, no dare, no how. We went about finding something else to do that day, but I can't remember what it was.

Over dinner, it was decided not to repair the old barn, but build a new, safer pole barn. Until then, we had to salvage what bales we could and stack them on the southern, stronger side of the barn.

Going to bed that night I thought how everything happened so slowly during the cave-in and how the rest of the day went by so fast. I went to sleep planning to recite the Lord's Prayer, but I am sure I didn't finish it. I drifted asleep right after I gave thanks for surviving another close call on the farm.

Trampled

A mean animal usually doesn't remain long on a farm. We had our share of sour personalities in livestock that, for some reason, just didn't like being domesticated and would seize every opportunity to take it out on the unaware.

A white pony named Mike was a patient and calculating example of a mean animal. He turned out to be a short timer with our small herd of horses.

He wasn't trained very well, and my eleven-year-old twin sister Amy took it upon herself to teach the pony to let her ride him bareback and advance his steering by teaching him how to neck rein, instead of plow reining. The difference being that with plow reining, the right rein is pulled back to go right, the left is pulled to turn left. This is used when walking behind the animal and the implement (say, a plow) is between you and it. To neck rein, the rein is brought against the neck on the opposite side of the direction you want to turn the animal. Neck reining frees a rider's hands and is a kinder, gentler way to guide the half-ton skittish beast under you.

Amy was confident she could teach Mike how to be a good riding pony. At an early age she had perfected her animal instructing technique by riding young sheep and old horses.

She would use baler twine and fashion a halter for the sheep, then, holding the twine taut, she climbed aboard the wide, flat back. The thick wool made for a comfortable seat, but keeping your balance was difficult because the skin of a sheep is typically three or four sizes too large. I'm sure the lamb's mother told it what Amy and I heard quite often from our mom, "You'll grow into it."

With Amy up, the sheep would stagger and run in the direction it was tipping. Because her feet could just reach the ground, Amy maintained her "seat," as they say in horse show circles, and was able to trail ride her Corriedale around the farmhouse. I know this because she showed me how to ride sheep too. It's a skill not practiced by many.

It was time for Mike to be home schooled. Amy and I had been floating corn-cobs in the horse trough again, pretending they were alligators. It was a mild summer day, the sun was bright and horseflies the size of June bugs buzzed around. The water tank and Amy were just inside the barnyard fence and I was on the outside. Mike had come across the barn-yard to see what we were doing, and Amy sensed a teachable moment.

"Go get the small bridle for me, I want to put it on Mike and ride him," Amy directed. She took the bridle, turned and walked to the pony. He edged away as usual and Amy started to work him into a corner by the corncrib. She turned to me to say something and the pony didn't hesitate, he jumped right at her, knocked her down and deliberately trampled her, a yellow hoof glancing off her head. We both yelled and Mike ran off to the pasture. Amy was sitting up, holding the top of her head, mad and crying.

She got up slowly and braced herself on the white painted corncrib. A fountain of red spurted from her head and spattered an arc three feet up the white washed boards. Then another spurt. It was a gusher.

"She's painting the barn!" I observed to older sister Patrice who had heard the commotion and was coming from the house. She started at the sight, turned and ran to get Mom while I opened the gate for Amy. My twin had both hands on her head, and running to the house as fast as her cowboy boots could take her.

Mom met her halfway up the walk. It was well known that our mother didn't tolerate the sight of her children's blood very well. I suppose it is something most mothers dread. She gasped, caught her panic in her throat and in a controlled voice told us to get in the station wagon; we're going to Dad's office.

To warrant a trip to "Dad's office" was about as bad as it got in terms of injury. Most kids feel bullet proof, but we had an edge in that when misjudgment prevailed and blood flowed, we could go to our Dad, a small town family physician and get patched up. My two older brothers, Patrice, Amy and I all have scars from wounds our father stitched closed.

Amy related how the injection of anesthesia made the back of her scalp feel cold while Dad sewed in ten small stitches.

Amy's scalp was still numb when plans for Mike unfolded. The number one idea was to shoot him and leave him in the pasture for the turkey vultures. This option had been exercised a year earlier on Patrice's billy goat that was posthumously convicted of eating a pair of Dad's goatskin (of all things!) work gloves.

"Give him to the army," I suggested. I had seen enough TV Westerns to know that dead army animals littered the prairie after every battle. "No, give him to the circus. When they see how mean he is, they'll feed him to the lions," calculated Amy.

Compassion prevailed and we gave Mike to a neighboring farmer. Over the years, when driving by, we'd see him in a big pasture, off by himself. Even other livestock shunned him. "Look, there's Mike," someone would chirp from the back seat. "That miserable!@#**#" would be the retort from the front seat.

To this day, Amy has a thumbprint sized dent in her skull and hair won't grow from the small patch of scar tissue, but she has a nifty close call on the farm to relate to her hair stylist.

Lightning Bolt,
Ball and Bounce

The farmhouse I grew up in was on a hill surrounded by oaks and hickory and was struck by lightning more than a few times. Of the seven oaks on our hill in 1960, only two remained after forty years. The others were struck by lightning and eventually came down.

Our family witnessed many strikes to the house or nearby. It was routine to gather in the family room when a spring blaster was coming in from the west. If things looked too threatening, we would head into the Michigan basement and walk on boards across the dirt floor to the southwest corner, near the two fuel oil tanks. The room smelled of oil and coal dust left over from coal burning furnace days.

One storm, that had all the makings of a tornado, had Mom, Dad, my two sisters and me taking refuge in this "safe room." Mom and Dad were craning their necks to look west through the small basement window and were watching the clouds roll in with the rain and wind. I was looking at them, and noticed that next to the small window frame was a fuel pipe coming from outside into the 250 gallon tanks.

It was made of metal, the outside pipe went four feet up the outside of the house and was wet and to complete my vision of horror, the twisted wire from the roof-top lightning rod was anchored within a few feet of it.

Having had the opportunity to experience a bolt or two, I'd read more about this violent force of nature. I recalled a picture of a house being struck. The photo caught the moment of the strike and how it went along the surface of the home into the ground stake.The caption said how the people in the home were protected by the lightning rod redirecting the bolt. "Well," I remember thinking, "That family didn't have the lightning blast into a room filled with fuel oil." I moved away and got behind my twin sister, who has a distinct and well-earned aversion to lightning storms.

We all feared getting hit by a bolt from above. It was part of being a kid. We couldn't help but jump every time we'd hear the "chik-bamBAMMM" of a bolt hitting nearby. Sitting on the living room davenport, we would raise our legs whenever thunder would start booming closer because our older brother Brad had told us how a lightning bolt takes the fastest way to Earth, and two feet planted on the ground made you a top choice.

Any gun-shy dog in the house would bolt into the room, scoot under our raised legs and hide under the sofa. The single-paned windows would rattle with every close blast.

One particularly threatening spring day, near sunset, a storm was coming and the air was still and thick with humidity. A ripe situation for a tornado and lightning. My two sisters and I were on the sofa next to Dad in his easy chair. Everything electrical was turned off and we were ready.

Our hair started to rise, just a little, and we knew what that meant. Up went our feet. Nothing. We had relaxed our legs for just a moment when a glow came from the kitchen and caught our attention.

A luminescent globe the size of a soccer ball floated through the middle of the kitchen doorway, halfway across the dining room table and paused above the silver plated cruet set of oils and vinegar. Our eyes were fixed on the scintillating white orb. The light was bright, not blinding, but certainly mesmerizing. It appeared to be deciding where to go. Our feet went up and the ball shot to the phone connection near the dining room table. The smell of ozone filled the room and I don't remember any thunder. It was eerily quiet, no buzzing or static popping. Was another one coming? Nobody moved, we were scared stiff.

After a minute, our fearless father got up from his recliner and walked into the dining room and inspected the telephone. It was not damaged but the line was dead. "That's what you call St. Elmos fire, I've heard of it, but never seen it before" he said.

We only witnessed St. Elmo's fire one more time over the years in that farmhouse. It, too, came from the kitchen sink, went over the table then it danced onto the living room floor beneath our raised feet before disappearing into an electrical outlet.

A neighbor claimed to have seen a ball of lightning jump crazily along the road to our driveway, then lift off and explode by a catalpa tree a hundred feet away. Not knowing that it was a phenomena called ball lightning, he told Dad it was bounce lightning and said it was heading for our house when it blew up as he drove by.

Naturally, we always stayed far away from the phone, kitchen and dining room when stormy weather threatened. As years went by, events like this, along with snakes in the basement, rats in the bathroom, and ghosts creeping up the stairs, diminished the number of safe retreats in that house.

Only recently have I learned the old

farmhouse has certain characteristics that make it attractive to electrical activity. The water well and its iron casing sink almost 300 feet, through gravel of quartz and granite, a salt water pool and then punches into a deep, hard water aquifer, not at all consistent with the soft water producing limestone upwellings of the area. Our little farmhouse on top of a hill was probably the most electrically conductive location for miles around.

That may explain the constant activity of our family household during my youth. We were always running on fully charged batteries.

Overcharged

My family had a fish tank in the dining room of our farmhouse during my preteen years. It sat next to the bathroom doorway on an antique dresser that had a grey and black flecked marble top but no mirror. Our house cats spent hours staring at the swimming temptations. The fish seemed oblivious to the cats, but would become quite agitated when the surface water was disturbed, as when sprinkling a flake or two of food upon it. The little air pump was behind the tank and puttered merrily along, air bubbles rising from the sunken deep-sea diver tipped over onto the green granules of the tank bed. It was a late afternoon on a Sunday and I was watching the fish and waiting for the bathroom to become available.

I decided to feed the fish and reached to turn on the light. I was watching the fish and not my hands and knocked the light into the tank. I felt a shaking grip on my hand and arm. My teeth clenched together with the alternating current hammering my 80 pound body in staccato pulses. I was in the grip of the electric current and could not get away.

The room looked fuzzy. My eyes were wiggling, most likely 60 twitches per second in phase with the alternating current. I couldn't let go. Dad opened the bathroom door and seeing my condition, knocked me away with a sweep of his arm. He ripped the plug from the outlet and looked at me.

I was knocked back a few steps and stood a moment, my mind and body settling down. "Can you hear me? Are you all right?" he asked as he evaluated me. "I can't believe the fuse didn't blow," he said looking back at the tank, the fish lazily swimming about the light fixture in the cloudy water.

We checked the fuse box in the basement. The screw-in fuse was vintage. "You know, this fuse has never blown and I'm sure lightning has nailed it a few times," said Pop as he flipped the arm of the fuse box up to shut off the power to it. He used needle-nose pliers to break the ceramic glass fuse and get at the metal threads, now arc welded to the grey metal box. He twisted away, and extracted the crumbling fuse from its socket. The fuse hadn't blown as much as melted together. Later that day, he announced his plan to rewire the farmhouse. "It doesn't make sense to have a pole barn with a better electrical system than our house," he declared and began the project that would last for weeks.

The electrical system of our house was in need of upgrading. In the kitchen, there was a hazard between the stovetop and kitchen counter. The vinyl counters edges were trimmed in chrome and if an unsuspecting cook leaned against it and touched the stove, he or she would get a jolting dose of 220 volts. This would cause the cook/victim to convulse and in so doing, break the circuit.

The kitchen's short circuit was first discovered, along with a couple of new epithets, during a holiday crowded kitchen. To put our concern in perspective, we had all seen lightning explode from the kitchen across the dining room enroute to the telephone outlet, so an arm numbing shock was a threat that was respected but not overly feared.

My two brothers' bedroom, fourteen feet square had two outlets. One by the light switch near the door, and another above the baseboard twenty feet away. The boys had a 45 rpm record player and desk lamp plugged into it. It was all the juice they needed. But times were changing and more, safer power was needed. Dad had gained enough experience with the pole barn project and felt confident he could handle the work.

The man on a mission crawled into places none of us had explored in the farmhouse. The attic above the bedrooms had no access until he made one. My sisters and I speculated on what he would find up there. A Civil War stash of rifles was my hope. Or gold and silver. Instead he found shovels full of squirrel gnawed acorns, walnuts and dried dog food, along with the resultant rodent created guano.

The two girls and I helped when we could. Dad let me shine the flashlight on his work, but at times, I would stare into the darkness and the light would drift off the field of operation. "Pay attention to what you're doing," was his standard response. The wiring was upgraded a circuit at a time, leaving parts of the house in the dark for days.

It was frustrating work by himself. Dropped tools disappeared into the blown insulation or into the darkness between wall studs. Sharp clipped wire poked his fingers. Accidental shocks followed by highly charged verbal outbursts reached a level that drove us out of the house.

Standing in the moonlit yard with our dogs, looking at the dark two story farmhouse and hearing startled oaths and threats course from it, we talked of visiting Mom's Uncle Floyd, who lived on a self-sufficient farm with no electricity.

"You know," said Mom as she crossed the yard and got into the stationwagon,"since we have to live without electricity anyway, we might as well go see what it's like on a farm that is used to it, and besides, it will probably be quieter," she hoped as we piled in behind her.

Tree Top Travelers

Tall, skinny maple trees shot up along the banks of lowland drainage ditches around the farm. My neighbor and blood brother, Larry Cobb and I would climb these trees and spend windy May afternoons moving through their treetops.

The drainage ditches were bordered on both sides by four to eight foot tall mounds of spill left when the dredges made them years ago, and the maples took over in the fresh, mucky soil, uninhibited and well watered for most of the seasons.

Within years they shot up forty feet or more from narrow ten to eighteen inch bases. They were as limber as the graphite tent poles used today. They shaded out any undergrowth, so only tangled maple branches and leaves littered the maple groove floor, and it was soggy when not under a few inches of water.

Larry and I would enter the dark kingdom at ground level and move through it from one tuft of sod to another, stepping to a fallen branch or onto crossed twigs to keep our boots from sinking in and gulping water. We held low branches to keep our balance and stayed far enough away to not be whipped in the face when the one ahead let go of a bow-bent limb.

One morning in May, with high cotton clouds skittering along with the spring wind, Larry and I walked in from the road, leaving our bikes just off the roadway on the downslope to the woods. Larry stopped by an area with scattered broken windshield glass and marveled at the reflecting colors and uniform size of the nuggets. "These are diamonds, we should fill our pockets and get rich," he joked. We didn't touch anything, though. The accident that left the glass had killed the early morning driver in February of that year. The ground and the struck tree were haunted. From a few yards away we would study the artifacts the police and wrecker left at the death scene. It took three years for raspberries and saplings to grow over it.

The waterways would be almost dry by football season, but during the spring, they were impossible to cross by most orthodox means. Our adventures would take us to the wormy banks of the ditch, lined with silent, gray columns of maples. In contrast, the treetops would swirl wildly in the changing May winds and clack and smack, letting fly bark and twig.

Our maneuvers were checked short by a moat filled with dark, mapleleaf tea water, our choices were crossing on a blown-down tree or taking the high way.

The high way was crossing over on a treetop to the other side. There is a certain point, when climbing a sapling, where it begins to bend. By positioning yourself properly, the top heavy maple would arch across the ditch and come up against the main trunk of a second maple affording a moment for a safe dismount. A risky and obvious choice for us.

After a few crossings we gained the confidence that ebbs and flows through four-teen-year-olds, and declared that touching the ground was taboo. The game was on to see how far you could go up one side of the ditch-bank, cross and bend your way back.

Without the proper precautions, such as the correct angle of attack, there was a high risk of having your knuckles rapped by the tar-get tree. My grip was tested more than once by a stationary limb as I bent into it. You had to try for a branch at the last moment. Not a lot of second chances at twenty feet up.

As spring turned to summer, climbing became second nature to us. A tall and most challenging tree was near Larry's house. The old poplar tree bordered a rich organic muck field. Four trunks grew to leafy tops fifty or sixty feet over the black, soggy field. There were no other trees near it. Up we went. Larry climbing one trunk, me up another. I climbed so high the temperature changed and I could see barns and silos miles away. The wind was creating a lot of noise as it will with poplar leaves. Larry had to shout to me from twenty feet away, but just as far up, "Come on over!" he laughed. I started to bend his way but the wind had other ideas. I was out of my element and at the mercy of the wind. The trunks bent like fishing rods with Larry and me suddenly hanging in space. The wind slowed and the tree straightened. We both retreated down the trunk to safer ground.

We stared at each other, slack jawed and wide eyed. Why one of those trees didn't snap was a wonder to us. Our little bodies would have disappeared into the muck like coffee stir-sticks into oatmeal. We never went up that tree again.

Brad, Todd and aircraft prior to test flight.

Brotherly Love and Free Fall

My oldest brother Todd once talked our brother Brad into jumping out of a second story barn window to see if he could fly. It was the first test flight of Todd's freshly made canvas wing. The boy wonder would come up with some harebrained idea and then start the project, using various materials scavenged from around the farm. He was a most resourceful young man.

In an earlier project during the late 1950s, Todd had dug a bomb shelter. He had been taught the "duck and cover" in school and been eager to share with the family how to survive a nuclear attack. Todd's dinnertime descriptions of melting flesh and blinding fireballs in the sky often put a damper on the rest of the family's more cordial conversations.

"I rode my horse bareback with only a halter and baler twine for reins," older sister Patrice had offered over mashed potatoes and gravy.

"If an atomic bomb went off over the capitol, the blast would boil our eyes in their sockets and our skin would be barbequed," Todd countered. "Our only hope is to have a bomb shelter, and I'm gonna make one this weekend."

He did such a good job of it, Dad encouraged him to enlarge it to accommodate the rest of the family. Todd built it facing our good friends and neighbors. He said he wanted to be able to watch their home vaporize from the safety of his shelter.

One winter and into spring, he busied himself in the basement, working on a rowboat that would double as a duck blind and carp hunting barge. It was a beauty. Glued, nailed, sealed with pitch, painted, varnished and too big to maneuver through the doorway at the top of the steps. We made a fine set of shelves with the green lacquered wood.

He wasn't one to dwell on failure. With all the material resources of a working farm and his unfettered imagination he was always in the middle of creating something, usually dangerous. If it burned fuel, all the better.

Then there came the flying contraption he built from regular wood, not the balsa wood he used to make his scale model boats and planes. The "wings" were made using an old saddle cinch, canvas liberated from an old army cot, and barn wood scraps. Todd was confident he had fashioned the wings to make a human fly, but to be sure he wanted middle brother Brad to jump from the neighbor's high barn window and test fly them. Word of the pending maiden flight spread through the neighborhood like last summer's outbreak of pink-eye. Brad couldn't chicken out now. A dozen kids from five farms gathered at ground zero, and craned their necks to look up at Todd in the barn peak opening, counting down to take off. 3-2-1. Brad had a brief moment of success, followed by accelerating failure. He crashed onto the milk house roof, ten feet below.

"That gives me an idea," Todd said, looking down at his writhing brother, "I'm gonna get a bed sheet and make a parachute."

Long Portage, Short Voyage

Every spring, snowmelt filled the drainage ditches along roads and fields to new levels and tempting new dangers. The skies were clear one fateful April Saturday and the weather had warmed into the low 50s. These conditions prompted my older sister Patrice to use the swollen water channels to practice her navigation and portage skills. The naval exercises started with her enlisting her younger twin siblings, Amy and me, to help with everything except the thinking. The first order of the day was to obtain a vessel.

"It holds water, so we know it doesn't leak, and it is big enough for the three of us, so that makes it just right," self-commissioned Admiral Patrice observed as we gathered by the horse watering trough in the barnyard.

Our ship was a barn-red galvanized metal water tank, almost as tall as nine-year-old Amy and me and four feet long with rounded ends. It took all of us to tip it over. The water gushed away and spooked the horses that had arrived to investigate, "Or maybe to get a drink," I surmised out loud. Our Admiral suggested that it would be good for me to learn the chain of command and shut up.

"Okay, you two get under it, we'll pretend you're a giant turtle following me to the ocean,"

Patrice said. She was always eager to engage her younger siblings in a scheme that meant work for us and fun for her, no doubt a skill she learned from our two older brothers.

Amy and I stumbled through the barnyard, past toe-bruising rocks and various styles and amounts of animal waste. Patrice kindly opened the gate and guided us through, "Just like a ship going through the Soo Locks!" she observed, then banged on the sides.

We turtled down the driveway, then right onto the road for a hundred yards to a drainage ditch swollen with ice water. Last year's marsh grass lay flattened along the banks, its yellow blades in contrast with the pewter-colored water. Styrofoam cups floated over a number of sunken cans, bottles and a winter's worth of litter. We pushed the tank partially into the water and held it fast. Being the lightest, Amy boarded first. She steadied herself, and I came aboard. Patrice came on deck amidship and pushed away, declaring, "To the equator!"

The poor to nonexistent seafaring charac-teristics of a flat-bottomed water tank, top heavy with three landlubbers, somewhat abbreviated our commander's inaugural speech.

We tipped and while shockingly cold water shipped in, we shipped out, everyone for himself. The tank settled on the bottom as we clawed and scrambled up the bank to the road. We regrouped on the road, water dripping from our clothes onto the pavement. "How are we gonna get that back to the barnyard before Dad comes home?" Amy asked between chattering teeth.

We ran home, our boots sloshing and sucking with each step. We undressed on the back porch and went inside to put on dry clothes and, with heat, change our skin color.

We salvaged the ship and our hides, using baler twine and a hay-hook that looked a lot like the iron hooked hand of a pirate. Patrice considered another go of it, only this time she proposed that we empty the fifty-five gallon steel drum of farm fuel and "Ride it like a hippo."

Amy and I knew better and left her to go float corn cobs in the horse trough as it filled with swirling water from the hose. We pretended they were alligators and, we felt, much safer than our older sister.

The stinking pile of sopping wet clothes had to be explained. For some reason, Mom and Dad weren't too upset with us, a reaction not all that rare. Perhaps the joy of their children surviving another close call on the farm outweighed the urge for them to take advantage of an educational moment.

SUMMER

Queenie, Dog of Legend

I received a social network bonus of a pleasant memory when a pet was mentioned in a comment to one of my status updates. I had to pause a moment and enjoy a reflection back to a dog that shared my youth in the 1970s.

She wasn't my pet. The walker/beagle cross was the family hunting dog of our neighbors, who lived a half-mile from the end of the driveway of our farm.

Her name was Queenie, and she was the whole package. What some dog handlers call a "Once in a lifetime" dog. She was a sweet and fearless dog, eager to please and hunt.

Queenie was beautiful. She was a mostly black, long legged, tricolor with a brown and white face with a feminine beauty, fine structure and big brown, trusting eyes.

Her master and my best friend, Larry Cobb hunted pheasants over her and always managed a shot or two in those years. "Oh yes, she only barks on roosters," Larry would claim after watching a ring-neck blast off in front of her.

Over many seasons Larry, Queenie and I hunted, hiked and explored the four sections of land surrounding our homes. She stayed close and would look back at us, checking in to see if we wanted her to "bust a brush pile" or hunt in a different direction.

The dog could run rabbits. She would bawl and dash along the track, stop, give voice again and scoot along, running the critter right back to us. She would trot up to Larry approvingly after hearing the blang from his .410 single.

Same thing with squirrels. Only the hound would run a squirrel up a tree, scratching up the trunk and whining earnestly as the bushytail dashed up out of danger, corkscrewing around the trunk to evade the attacker.

Queenie would then drop to all fours, circle and spook the squirrel to our side and into our rifle sights. Putting a raccoon up a tree was simple to her. I didn't coon hunt, as Larry's older brothers or father would hunt late into the night, but I could hear her sounding along the track or the higher pitched, urgent call when the game retreated up a tree. I could lie in my bed and listen to her baying, fading in and out along with my bedside AM radio, tuned to the Canadian station, CKLW.

Her nose became legend one summer day, when her loyalty drove her from her house to be with Larry and me.

We were going fishing, and Queenie wasn't invited. Larry left her in the house so she wouldn't follow him as he rode his bike to my place. Enroute to the lake, we walked through our pasture, flipping cowpies to gather the wiggly red worms beneath. Arriving at the dock we tipped the rainwater from the boat and pushed off, crossing the lake to a spot that seemed promising.

It was a hot day, with fluffy clouds and an occasional breeze that would pivot the small boat a few degrees along the anchor line.

Buzzing dragonflies, blackbirds, muskrats, water snakes and the tempting twitch of a bobber kept us occupied. After a while, I noticed a distant, growing V in the water coming from our put-in spot.

"Look, a snake or a muskrat is swimming our way," I pointed out to Larry, who turned and squinted a look. "No-- that's Queenie!" he blurted.

In a few minutes she made the boat and we lifted her in, ending her two mile odyssey. "She tracked me down the road, through the farm, and then tracked me across the water! Isn't she the greatest dog in the world?" crowed Larry.

That day, under a summer sun many dogs ago, there was no doubt.

Children in a Tumbler

For the ranging pack of kids growing up in my farm neighborhood of the 1960s, the bigger the toy the better. One of the biggest was a wooden telephone wire spool modified for outdoor entertainment.

A neighbor worked for the phone company and on occasion, brought home empty wooden spools once wrapped with telephone wire. With five kids, Mr.C was sure the spools would find some use, if not as a garage poker table. A company truck was needed to drop off the biggest we ever saw. The behemoth had wheels six feet tall and made of wood planks cross-hatched four inches thick.

The old wooden spool was held together with rusty iron bolts and nuts. The unfinished surface was a constant source of splinters for us. We tipped it onto the wheels and started it rolling down our sledding hill. It gained speed and continued deep into the tall weeds that would have stopped a riding lawn mower.

Larry, Amy, Ritchie and I rolled the new found ride up the hill. Ritchie mounted the spool and stood between the wheels like a Roman charioteer. He started down the hill and looked up at us as he ran in place for almost four rotations. He was holding his own until the spool bounded from under him. He fell to the weeds screaming "Geronimo," landed on his feet and fell over, thrashing and claiming in a high pitched scream he broke his leg. Amy screamed "Jam pile" and bounded ahead of Larry and I down the hill and piled onto him. Before Larry and I could make our own leap to complete the jam pile, the victim displayed evidence of complete healing. Now at full strength, we righted the spool and pushed it up the hill once again.

By knocking out one of the center spindle boards, we wedged easily into the opening. It was our plan to then roll downhill, gaining speed and airtime. If only the Greeks had this, we agreed, they wouldn't have needed a big wooden horse waiting outside the gates of Troy. The soldiers could have crashed through the gates rolling along inside one of these juggernauts.

It was decided the best ride would be inside the center spindle. There was plenty of room for a test pilot. We looked around, the hunting dog, Queenie, who possessed the highly refined sense of knowing what Larry or Ritchie were thinking, moved nervously out of sight behind the garage. That left a semi-domesticated barn cat reclining in the shade.

The spool was tipped onto the wheels and the animal, demonstrating a great deal of resistance, and little bladder control, was inserted.

With a slight push, the maiden flight began down the hill. The wood and bolts rattled as the rolling spool tipped onto one wheel and gained speed. It bumped and the cat shot out and up into the air, a twisting and clawing blur of gray fur.

After landing, our test pilot hero bolted in high gear through the weeds. The speed of the parting foliage was looked upon as a good sign that the animal was unhurt. Since the cat apparently had not been killed or maimed, the test was declared a success.

Next in, after drying out the inside of the spindle, went my dear twin Amy and myself. We leaned our backs against the wheel ends of the spindle, facing each other. Dandelion-sized clumps of cat fur hung from the splinters and exposed bolt ends inside our capsule. We braced ourselves with our hands as we turned.

As we gained speed, so did the severity of the jolts and bumps. Amy and I lost our grips. We tumbled into each other with an increasing frequency of collisions. The most painful convergences were the head to head, followed by head to wood and then elbow to head.

Larry and Ritchie, standing at the crest of the hill observing our run, heard our nervous giggles turn to shouts of alarm and then to screams of pain. The child mix master came to a stop, and Amy and I extricated ourselves. We stood rubbing our heads and checking for blood on our clothes. After full-contact activities, it was important to find blood stains on your clothes and spit on them to keep a stain from setting.

The boys came running down, laughing. "Man, we're so glad you guys went first!" they hooted.

Ritchie and Larry, acting on our test flight recommendations, hammered the bolt ends over and clipped the splinters flush with the unfinished wood surface. In went Larry, and his design contribution, two of his mom's sofa pillows. He braced himself in the middle of the spindle and managed a blood-free ride, though he did sustain a goose egg to his forehead. Next in was Ritchie. He added a football helmet and mouth guard and had the best ride of all.

As with most of our homemade contraptions, the development of safety procedures was a rare and painstaking process. Within our gang of neighborhood kids, hare-brained ideas grew quickly into breakable, flammable, crashing prototypes. Only after blood loss was attention given to potentially lethal details.

After a painful crash into a tree we moved on to other less bruising diversions. The cable spool kid tumbler, despite providing consistently high levels of adrenalin and near-death experiences, was soon repurposed.

Similar advancements in automotive safety led the industry to develop crash test dummies. I can only imagine the number of close calls we could have avoided if we'd had a busload of those.

Doc's Docking Lessons

The month of March on most farms is a time of births. My brother Brad raised sheep and the experienced ewes would give birth, usually to twins, during the month.

Sheep are not known for being smart, combining their IQ with those of chickens would most likely not break double digits. New mamma sheep that give birth to a single baby sometimes would not accept the lambs as their own. When this happened, whoever was doing the chores would tuck the newborn under their winter coat and carry them into the farmhouse. The lamb was examined, iodine was doused on the belly button and the patient nestled into a cardboard box and placed next to the heat register near the kitchen sink cabinet. A day or two after surviving their first close call, off they went to a stall in the barn with other orphans.

If the lamb had been exposed to the elements for a few hours and was not moving easily or could not get up, Dad would mix a shot of whiskey and milk formula in a pop bottle with a soft rubber nipple for the baby to nurse. This usually helped them relax and fall asleep.

My siblings applied this remedy on more than one occasion to a house pet, cats being a favorite "patient." One rowdy calico kitten was given the milk cocktail in a bowl. We looked on as a tentative lick was followed by rapid lapping. The critter appeared to take a liking to the concoction. Moments later the kitty staggered away, until encountering the basement steps where it descended without benefit of using each one. Concerns for the fur ball's health were abated when inspection of the dreamy eyed kitty revealed a purring and unhurt feline. "Maybe it's something we could use at bedtime for the twins?" wondered oldest brother Todd during our early years in the 1960s.

Having a wee animal baby in the house was a welcome chore for my twin Amy and older sister Patrice. The two had bottle fed infant red squirrels, baby birds, skunks, kittens and puppies using a doll's bottle and nursed to health foals and lambs using a green quart Squirt bottle. Feeding lambs would wiggle their long tails and root against the nipple, all to the delight of the girls holding the ripple-sided glass pop bottle. Just hearing the powdered formula bag open would cause the little sheep to run and jump and tangle between the girl's feet in hungry anticipation.

As the lambs grew and the days lengthened and warmed, a date was set to dock their tails and castrate the males. Brad would close the barn doors, keeping the flock with the thirty or so lambs inside. The youngsters were dropped into the orphan pen and the worrying mothers would be driven out of the barn. Dad and my brothers would go to work. The lambs would be gently held and rear ends presented for the medical doctor.

Using a broad-nosed surgical tool from his office, Dad would crimp the three inch wide clamp onto the tail at the first joint effectively severing the nerves. After a moment to allow the crushed blood vessels to constrict, he removed the clamp. With a quick stroke using a fresh scalpel across the crease, he sliced off the tail and tossed it to the waiting dogs.

While the shocked lamb was still bleating, a brother would squirt iodine on the stub, steady the lamb and let go. We'd watch the new short tail for a few minutes to make sure the bleeding had stopped before moving on to the next one.

The male lambs got extra attention. After their tails were trimmed, the little boys were placed on their backs and the wide nosed clamp was crimped onto their thimble-like extra accessory that housed a pair of sensitive "items." This often caused a higher pitched bleat that would make my brothers and I wince in sympathy.

Dad would often use this occasion to bring up a few things that needed correction. Today's teachers would call this an educational moment.

"It sure would be nice if you guys put my tools back when you were done with them," Dad would say as he crimped down, the lambs plaintive bleat accentuating his point.

"Why don't you guys put gas in the car after using it?" he asked while deftly slicing away, then pressing down on the surgical field to expose what looked like two white Good and Plenty candies. Another slice, a toss and then one of us would fill the newly vacated pouch with iodine. Dad threw in a stitch or two using cat gut pulled by a curved needle held by surgical hemostats. The flat-nosed scissors with ridged tips locked together for a secure grip in the bloody environment.

The little fellas walked a bit bow legged after their neutering, but within a few days were gamboling with their bob-tailed cousins in the pasture.

Following a few of these operations, Dad would offer to trade places with one of us. "See one, do one, teach one," he repeated from his medical school days. When we finished cleaning up, the broad-nosed crimp was hung on a nail in the barn next to a crowbar and grease gun that were, not surprisingly, always put back after use. After forty-five years the clamps are still there, waiting in the now silent barn for the next docking day.

Dad Overboard

Probably the most exciting time my Dad ever had angling on our farm's lake was when he was the one being fished for.

One muggy August in the 1960s, when Mom and the rest of us were visiting Grandma and Grandpa overnight, Pop decided it was a good time to go fishing. My Dad would some-times fish at night on the small lake on the north end of the property we shared with two other farms. He'd walk back to the lake along the tractor path, lightening bugs flashing by the hundreds in the humid, still evening over the low pasture land. He kept most of his gear in our tar-papered shack affectionately called the "hut" near our campsite on the lake. Dad could leave the kitchen, walk the half-mile path and be fishing in minutes.

Largemouth bass, panfish, bullhead, carp, and dogfish were plentiful as the lake was not fished that often. Dad pushed the boat into the water and paused on the dock to survey the lake, listening for the splash of feeding bass, muskrat, raccoon or bird.   He stepped into the boat with his tackle box that held thirty years' worth of collected baits and plugs. Old Heddon and Mepps lures and a new Rapala minnow along with a rusty-capped jar of pork rinds and classic red and white Daredevils and Silver Spoons of different sizes. He would fish a spot, then row to another location in his Sears Roebuck flat-bottomed aluminum boat.

For night fishing, a surface plug was the lure of choice. Dad would spin cast one of his favorite Jitterbugs and slowly retrieve the gurgling bait. The private lake was the most peaceful of places to be on the farm. It was occasionally fished by paying guests that came down a long tractor path from the neighboring farm on the northern end of the lake.

He was fishing the south end of the lake and getting some strikes. The fish stringer of the drifting boat hung up in the lily pads and he bent over the side to untangle it, causing the boat to flip, dumping everything into the black lake waters.

Bright and early the next morning, the third owner of the lake, Morris Price, rowed onto the lake in hopes for a quiet hour or so of fishing. The overturned boat immediately caught his attention and he made his way to it. Small bags of hooks were floating along with bobbers and some surface baits. The boat had flipped when someone was fishing from it, he determined and called out. No answer came and he looked about, now convinced that whoever had fallen out was not above the surface. He also recognized the boat as Doc Weddon's.

Morris hurried from the lake to the closer Beauchamp farmhouse. Before he finished his story, Mrs. Beauchamp had called the county sheriff's department. Within the hour, the serenity of the lake was overwhelmed by the wailing sirens of police and ambulance vehicles called in for a water rescue.

By this time, Dad had been in bed a few hours. After being dumped into the lake, he swam to the dock, only 50 moonlit yards away. He pulled himself onto the deck and let the water run off him. The woods echoed with his cursing. He hadn't lost his shoes, so he decided to make his way back to the farmhouse.

Getting the boat and retrieving his gear could wait until tomorrow's light.

As thick as the fireflies were in the night, their numbers paled in comparison to the clouds of mosquitoes that annoyed Dad on his gauntlet run/walk to the house. Apparently seething anger attracts them more than carbon dioxide and body odor.

When reaching home, he threw everything wet onto the back porch and went to bed still fuming. He was up and out of the house by midmorning, determined to recover all his gear.

As he approached the woods, he heard many voices coming from near the family campsite. Already in a less than jovial mood, he girded himself to deal with trespassers and stalked to the campsite near the dock, ready to unload. The voices were coming from the lake, so he walked out on the dock. "What the hell is going on here?" he asked a young deputy in a boat 20 feet away.

"Doc Weddon's boat sank and we think he drowned," he said. Before Dad could say anything, Morris called from a sheriff's boat, "Is that you Doc? My gawd, we're dragging the bottom for you!"

"Let me know if you find anything! I hope you at least get my tackle box," he retorted, his anger softening to a chuckle.

The much relieved officers brought the boat and oars to the dock and after some back-slapping and retelling of the capsizing, they were on their way.

Dad collected what he could along the lakeshore and left the rest on the lake bottom. If he had to dive for the stuff, he wanted someone in a boat to help.

Later that afternoon, I went with him to continue the salvage operation. It turned out to be more dangerous than his close call the night before.

Sunset over the scene of the water recovery.

Bugged Eyed and Breathless
(continued from Dad Overboard.)

One sunny, Sunday afternoon in August in the 1960s, my sisters and I were in the family station wagon with Mom at the wheel, heading home after visiting our grandparents overnight.

Dad was home on the farm, tinkering on the tractor, looking for the side-cutters I hadn't put back. Small chores that would only take minutes with the proper tool could drag out for hours when he had to look for hammer, saw or pliers, which was most of the time.

Between my older brothers and me, most of his tools had left the safety of his tool box long ago and were scattered around the farm.

At least we were enjoying a peaceful, beautiful Sunday drive. Our frustrated Dad was talking out loud to himself and the barn cats. Mom drove up the driveway and continued to near the back door and parked. We boiled out on a run, calling firsts for the lone bathroom in our four bedroom farmhouse.

Mom relayed how her mom and dad were and summarized our behavior report to Dad. He then explained how his boat tipped over and his tackle box and rod and reel had sunk to the bottom of the lake. He wanted me to go with him to help get his gear.

We rode the tractor to the lake. At the start of a long flat stretch of lane, Dad would put the Ford Powermaster into road gear and our speed would really pick up. I'd ride with my ten-year-old frame between his seat edge and the left rear wheel fender. I'd prop myself on the fender facing him, my two hands gripping the rim on either side of me, one foot on the big red axle, the other braced on the upper connection of the three-point hitch.

We flipped the boat over and pushed it into the lake, pulled it alongside the dock and carefully stepped in. "Watch it when you get in," Dad cautioned me as we stepped into the three seat Myers aluminum boat. "Flat bottomed boats like this can flip really fast, so be careful," he stressed.

We were both going to dive for stuff on the bottom, or pick lures from the weeds and lily pads. I was searching the reedy shoreline. "It was right here, I'm sure of it," said Dad as he pulled up his oars. I immediately looked down from the front of the boat. Near the bottom, eight feet below, was a golden monster of a carp. I could see fish scales as big as gold doubloons glinting in the late afternoon sun attached to a tail the size of my baseball glove. The fish glowed yellow and fiercesome to me. I watched it effortlessly disappear into the shadows beneath a line of lily pads. I turned to my dad and declared "I'm not going into the water with that."

"With what? What did you see?" asked my dad. "A fish almost as big as me-- it just swam from under our boat to those lily pads," I stammered. Dad was silent as he slipped the anchor into the water and tied it off. "OK, I'll dive and when I come up, I'll hand stuff to you," he offered and it suited me just fine.

Over he went with a splash and a boat rising ripple. He brought up a reel first, then back down he went. He brought up his rod and reel, the bait still snug at the tip. "Have to be careful not to stir up the bottom," he spit while holding the side of the boat to catch his breath.

Our efforts became a rhythm of dive, select, surface. Dad swam like an otter. Things were going well.

Down he went. I counted to thirty, his usual span before breaching. I looked over the side and saw a cloudy plume of mucky water. Up from that came a large tackle box of a different color than my father's.

Dad had picked up the smaller items first, saving the box for last. He was a little played out, but stubbornly pushed himself for one more dive. After 40 seconds underwater Dad committed precious more to latching the lid closed before kicking for the boat, six feet up. He broke the surface two feet away and pushed the box toward me, going under with the effort.

A few hours in the cleansing waters of the lake had turned the old dark metal tackle box into a light shade of grey that my mind couldn't register as Dad's.

I stared at the bobbing box and was sure it wasn't his, so I didn't grab it. I didn't know Dad was under it, feet in the muck, holding it to the surface, turning blue.

The box slipped back into the murkiness and then surfaced again, jiggling up and down, water streaming from its corners.

The box sank and up came a bug eyed Dad, sucking air and looking at me in disbelief. He steadied himself with one hand and brought up his other, clenched around the handle of his tackle box. He tipped it into the boat and then pulled himself in.

"Why didn't you take the (insert expletive of choice here) tackle box?" he coughed. Black mucky water drained off him and the box.

"I didn't think it was yours," I explained, shrugging my shoulders.

"(insert another expletive of choice), I (add one more) near drowned getting that (one more) to the (last one) surface," he vented.

That was it for the salvage operation. It was the first time I was glad to leave the lake. It took a few retellings of Dad's weekend of close calls to gain the humorous perspective my siblings have today.

Hot Weather and Cold Blood

In the 1960s, air conditioned shopping malls were not yet the fashionable place to find relief from the humid Michigan July heat. For me and my circle of thirteen-year-old friends, afternoons in the shade of 150-year-old hickory and oak trees was the finest relief we could find.

Our campsite was on a raised area that looked eastward over a spring-fed lake. A pathway went from the campfire under the shady canopy, down the incline. As it approached the lake, old boards led the way over wet muck and past tall saw grass, then onto the wooden deck that went through cattails and out over the water. The dock was built on top of a former dock's frame, using many of the old posts and cross members for support. Practical for sure, but it left the most attractive habitat for snakes and muskrats.

Blue herons nested on the lake and hunted the shoreline. Sometimes they stood on the dock, waiting patiently for frogs or snakes. White, plate-sized splotches that looked like spilled paint testified to the success of the birds.

It was typical to see water snakes on the decking, not coiled but extended with heads held back on a cocked neck. As visitors, we would walk out to them and watch as they slopped sideways into the water and disappeared under the dock, slithering up onto a weathered plank of the old dock.

I would always be extra alert when approaching the dock for the initial time. The snakes were by far the largest snake on the farm. Blue racers may be longer, but these Eastern water snakes were at least twice as thick and far more aggressive.

While cooling off in the water, it was always a good idea to keep a sharp eye out for incoming snakes. Being the only structure on the lake, the dock was a beacon to every critter swimming from the other shore.

The first thing to do when seeing one swimming toward the dock, was to paddle behind somebody else in the water and then point past them and yell "Snake!" False alarms were frequent.

The snakes made much better speed on the water than I ever did. While treading water, I'd see one coming from fifty yards away, then swim like crazy back to the old ladder nailed to the dock, climb out and watch the snake arrive. Splashing didn't always drive the snakes away, sometimes they would just dive and become undulating shadows among the weeds.

An example of the snake's fearless nature was demonstrated one July on that dock.

My friend Mark and I walked from the farm to the lake for a little cane-pole fishing with worms. It was midday when we made the campsite. We set up the pole and dug some worms from the black muck. I was following Mark as he stepped up from the path onto the dock and stopped, pointing the pole. At the end of the dock was a pretty good sized water snake, most likely a female, lazing in the sun. We approached her with confidence that she was going flop off the dock. We weren't too keen on trying to catch her. When held, the snakes can excrete a tar colored foul, stinking liquid that doesn't wash off that easily. The odor is worse than springtime skunk.

The snake twitched when we were a cane pole length away. After giving us a good look, she tossed her head and sidewinded off the dock into the water below.

Mark and I stomped on the dock, just to make sure the big mama didn't wrap up on the older dock, inches below the boards we were on.

We traded using the pole. One of us would fish with the pole, lifting the panfish high out of the water and then swinging the catch to the other, who would unhook the blue gill and rebait as necessary. I was helping out, lying outstretched on my back with my hands behind my head. Mark was giving a report of the bobber's movements. I was relaxing with my eyes closed when I felt a cold tickle on my forearm. I swung my other arm over it, expecting to catch the fishing line. "Mark is dangling the worm right over me," I guessed, and put my arm back after it stopped.

Mark continued to speak and I felt it again. This time I turned my head and was eye to eye with that water snake. So close I could smell her breath. The thing was going to slither over my arm and was actually touching it with her wagging red tongue. I tensed so hard in fright, my body spun and I was on all fours in an instant. The snake recoiled and shot off to my left and into the water. By then I was on my feet with my heart in my mouth.

"I never saw it come onto the dock!" exclaimed Mark, now standing with me, looking to see where the snake went. "That snake was bigger around than your arm, it's huge!" he blurted.

We gave the large snake the name of Emil. One letter away from evil. She was seen regularly and was given the utmost respect. For some reason, she made the aluminum rowboat a favorite retreat. Emil would wait until the hapless person rowing the boat was most unaware before revealing herself from under the very seat the oarsman occupied.

This predictability came in handy. During a family get-together at the lake, a niece offered a boat ride to her high school friend. It was part of her helpful plan to desensitize her guest from a spastic fear of snakes.

The two young girls hadn't rowed too far from relatives on the dock and were yakking and laughing when Emil made her grand entrance. The friend levitated completely out of the boat and hit the lake's surface running. She made three steps across the lake before gravity took effect. A feat that St. Peter would have envied.

My niece, who was expecting a much smaller version of therapy, abandoned the ship to Emil. Her form on exiting was not perfect, but she did get a standing ovation from her uncles and aunts who witnessed the close call.

Hot Dogs and
Summer Camp Outs

"Camping Out," that's what we called it. What it really meant was freedom to cut loose in the great outdoors. My friend Larry and I spent many nights camping, mostly at the generations old campsite located in a woods next to a small, spring-fed lake one-half mile from the farmhouse. Hot summer nights were cooler there, and with nightfall, we were free to roam the open, moonlit fields of the farmland we had spent the better part of our thirteen years growing up on.

Camping out in the 1960s would be considered primitive today. For us it was one way to test our self-sufficiency. We would be out of touch of parents and older siblings and their constant attempts to be helpful in molding our youthful personalities. We would stay up late, eat junk food and disregard the high level of personal hygiene they demonstrated. As attractive as that was to us, we could only manage to escape to camp on a weekly basis, usually a Friday night. Even though we didn't work or have school, it seemed that neither of us could get our chores done and scavenge enough cash for supplies any sooner.

No planning ahead for us. We lived off the land and started our gleaning in the kitchen. Food was pilfered from the family refrigerator, matches from parents or the kitchen junk drawer and accessories such as firecrackers or bottle rockets from our older brothers' stashes.

In the 'fridge, leftovers in old cottage cheese containers were a favorite target. We couldn't see through the plastic, so opening them was somewhat thrilling. Finding one with cottage cheese in it was a pleasant surprise. Usually the sixteen ounce containers held leftover mashed potatoes, baked beans, jello or, one time, a fecal specimen for the vet. We laughed about that because we were sure it was my older sister's, so we wrote her name on it when we put it back in the vegetable drawer.

The ice chest in my house wasn't always full of high grade nutrition. It was impossible to fill with normal food because it was the only cold storage in the house. The old Frigidaire held a variety of items that needed to be kept cool. It wasn't unusual to reach past a jar of sheep or horse wormer for the milk. Shelves contained jars of waxworms, Tetanus and other vaccines, camera film and batteries, farm animal specimens and wild game. UFO's or Undated Frosty Objects occupied the freezer's corners, partially encased in 1950s ice.

Mom's fur coat project had two cleaned but unskinned road killed mink in the freezer. The two were the same species, but so many generations apart Darwin could have compared them to demonstrate evolutionary adaptation.

The older mink had a permanent grimace from his skin retracting up his snout due to the freeze drying effect of his final resting place. It was the first thing you saw when opening the freezer. It was an appetite killing device still untapped by the diet conscious crowd.

The pair of Saran-wrapped rodents would greet us when we opened the freezer to retrieve a birthday cake, unfinished from the last memorable milestone and frugally stored in the freezer for the next celebration. Those cakes had a half life longer than fruitcake, and were best enjoyed with plenty of ice cream piled on.

A school of ten, partially cleaned and frozen bluegills older than me hung motionless in a Wonderbread bag, all staring foggy-eyed in the same direction. "I know that look, they must be learning history in that school," I joked.

Larry and I grabbed what we could and jammed it all into a double brown paper grocery sack. A typical bag would contain a flashlight, AM radio, cans or bottles of pop, smashed hot dog buns, hot dogs, potato chips and a partially full jar of pickle relish with catsup and mustard already mixed in.

We didn't have insect repellent, but burned green leaves that created enough smoke to drive away the bugs and sometimes our dogs. For shelter, we had an army surplus green canvas pup tent. We both had sleeping bags, Barlow pocket knives and Daisey BB guns. We were ready.

Down the lane we gamboled, through the pasture and into the untamed north of the farm.

Our dogs stayed close, hanging near the one carrying the grocery sack. I was sure they were defending it, but Larry claimed they were waiting for it to drop so they could eat everything.

When Larry and I first started camping, the most forgotten item was toilet paper. Try as we might, we just couldn't remember to bring a roll. Our memories improved exponentially after an educational and upright ten days following a delicate encounter with poison ivy or poison oak. We never learned which for sure, as it was a nighttime double exposure.

Once a fire was started, we'd cut long

green sticks, impale a wiener, and cook hot dogs over the flames. Much like our ancestors around campfires of old, deep philosophical questions were examined. We buy hot dogs in ten packs, yet buns come only in eight packs? How come? Why don't dogs get poison ivy?

The dogs were on their own when it came to being fed. They eagerly accepted the challenge and waiting patiently for dropped or unattended food. We tolerated their begging. When night came, they would earn their keep. Often rushing from the light of the meager smoking campfire into the dark woods. Sometimes bolting off in silence, but mostly tearing off at the guttural and fiercesome sound of a boar coon or night heron.

Camping with Larry's older brother Ritchie was always a treat. He claimed to have taught tricks to the dogs. One such demonstration was destined to never be repeated. He held a raw hot dog at arms' length above the ground and commanded their dog Queenie to jump and she did, cleanly snapping the hot dog from his fingers. He did this a number of times with various placements of hot dogs about his person. It earned great laughs from me and Larry watching a dog bite a dog. Ritchie ran out of hot dogs and moved just to the edge of the campfire light to attend to a full bladder.

Apparently, Queenie didn't catch on that the show was over and jumped and snapped. Ritchie leaped back screaming, but intact.

The retelling of that close call became standard fare for the rest of our shared campfires.

FALL

The Sandbox

Our farm had a sandpit dug by my brothers. It was made during their attempt to create a beach on the mucky shores of a lake that two other farms shared with ours.

Teenage brothers Todd, Brad and their friend Darryl dug and pitched sand onto the flat hay wagon for most of one morning and then backed it down the lane with the tractor to the small wooden dock and shoveled it off. By the end of the day, the three had moved a couple of dump truck amounts of sand that made a small sandy patch in the tall cattails next to the dock. They had been inspired by the current wave of beach blanket teen movies. "All we need now are some girls in bikinis," said Brad wistfully.

From time to time throughout that summer, the boys did recruit some to their beach, but the sandscape disappeared a little more after every summer downpour. The mosquitoes didn't do much for their other plans either and in a few years, black muck once again surrounded the planks we walked onto the dock.

The pit remained and was a source for light brown sand. With all that material available, Dad decided to make a sandbox for the six-year-old twins.

He used three large planks and the eastern side of our wooden framed milkhouse for the fourth side. Short boards were nailed across the corners to make small seats and provide bracing for the square frame. Two pear trees flanked the little shed, providing shade and a gathering spot for sparrows. The sandbox became a favorite playspace. On hot days, Amy or I could always dig down in the deep sand to cool earth.

We had many toy horses made of solid plastic that roamed our little desert and dunes in search of adventure or escape. Blue, gray and green Civil War or WWII style toy soldiers and cowboys marched and disappeared in the shifting sands. A number of toy tractors and trucks and most of the serving spoons from the kitchen were in there somewhere.

One challenging pastime was burying a dime and then using a scribbled map to find it. Despite the creative drawings and arrows with X marking the spot, it was not an easy task. Sand would fly as we searched franticly for the silver ten cent piece. It was enough money to buy a pop and a candy bar so we were motivated.

Ripe pears dropped in and around the sandbox and attracted red squirrels, hornets and yellow jackets. Despite these natural barriers, Mom would suggest that we collect the pears that had not yet been claimed to make pear jam. She didn't like to see things go to waste. This frugality rubbed off on Brad and Todd and they repurposed a few rotten pears of their own. The two made pear grenades by stabbing a firecracker into the rotting fruit. The fuse was lit and at the right moment, tossed to explode in the air over friend or barnyard.

It was a high traffic play area for Amy and me and the cats. The first thing we did when stepping into the sandbox was to check for scratch or pug marks made by cat or twin. It was pretty easy to track down and uncover the tootsie roll like blessings left behind.

A kid had to be careful on the farm. I learned the importance of planning ahead by walking barefoot. Picking glass, manure and pricker free landings for my next few steps was critical. When chased by animal or family and needing speed, an entire escape route had to be visualized, much like today's free style climbers planning each handhold up a cliff, but with more urgency.

Digging with tools or bare hands could move lots of sand, but for rapid excavations, the garden hose delivered the most excitement. With enough water, we were able to pan for gold and uncover ancient ruins of red plastic hotels and green houses that dated back to the times of Marvin Gardens and Park Place.

Taking note of our lounging cats, Amy and I borrowed a blue and white enamel roaster for an inground cat pool. We thought the water and sandy beach was just right for cooling them off on a hot day, but our feline friends were unappreciative and clawed their way out of those close calls.

Twin Air Bags

Air bags are standard safety equipment in today's cars. I was lucky to have the same protection years before even seatbelts were standard safety equipment.

A good example of this future technology was demonstrated one March day in the driveway of my family farm in the 1960s. I was riding our Shetland pony, Midget, when he decided to scrape me off his back by rubbing against the mailbox post. As luck would have it, I was riding double and bareback, behind my twin sister Amy. She was an excellent rider by the time we were twelve and could handle a stubborn and mean pony.

The mailbox was just the right height to clear his back and bump into Amy and me. I could have been seriously hurt if it wasn't for my personal airbag, my dear twin. I made it a point to always have Amy up front when riding double. Midget had other tricks that made this a good move. We'd be trotting along when he'd suddenly stop and drop his head. Amy and I would slide halfway down his neck when he would flinch and off we'd go. Amy would hit the ground and I would land on her, breaking my fall. Midget would stop a few feet away, just out of reach, and look back at us.

Amy was a cushion for indoor activities as well. The starcase was the scene of many downhill races on pillows. Pillows became the vehicle of choice after Patrice, Amy and I surfed down the steps on a mattress, lost navigational capabilities and bludgeoned each other with knee and skull.

Riding double on a pillow can slow it down, but having Amy in front was worth it. My older sister would position herself behind the stairway door to the living room and close it just as we were going our fastest down the stairs. We had to grab the handrail at the last moment to keep from slamming headlong into the door.

Yes, I was lucky. When riding with Amy between me and trouble, I was saved from doorknobs, mailboxes, thorn trees, fence posts, tractor wheels, and driveway gravel laced with clinkers from the old coal furnace.

I kept this practice going even when camping in the farm woods. I would put her sleeping bag between me and the tent flap, just in case a wild panther attacked while we slept. The plan was for Amy to slow it down while I ran for help.

Badger next to Alex with his first shotgun and a cottontail. Behind the two hunters is Max, the Bittany spaniel. photo by Willah Weddon

My Weapons
from Birth to Age Ten

When I was ten years old in the mid-1960s, I acquired my brother's hand-me-down BB guns. They were a fine addition to my pint-sized collection. My first gun was a toy double-barreled cork gun. The corks had two-foot lengths of string stapled to them and secured to the rib below the barrels. Each barrel had its own trigger and made a delightful "blat" when fired. I was only four but remember the first time I listened to an LP record of Prokofiev's "Peter and the Wolf." I was holding the album cover and saw that the little boy Peter was carrying the same cork gun as I had. It was an immediate bond. We were kindred spirits, and from then on I have enjoyed classical music and woodwinds.

By age five, I grew into cap guns. I had cap revolvers, semiautomatics, rifles and a red plastic rocket with a metal nosepiece that slammed into a cap on impact, making a decent crack about every other throw.

I never had enough red paper rolls of caps. The rolls were like a perforated tape with little pimples of black powder between holes that were spaced down the middle. Green peel and stick individual explosive caps were used in my revolvers and fanning off six shots took far less time that it did to load the caps and bullets. I enjoyed the smell of burnt powder. And was always on the look out for another cap gun.

Grocery stores had toys hanging at the end of the aisles, and I would survey them with great interest from my position on the bottom rack of the shopping cart. Mom would push it along, my twin Amy in the cart's kid seat, facing her and carrying on conversations that started with "I want…"

On this day, I was secured into position beneath a half-full basket. Time was running out, there were only a couple of aisles to go before checkout so I redoubled my recon.

There were cough drops and remedies at the end of one aisle, and an attractive cigarette offer on the next, but sure enough, my vigilance paid off, just down the last aisle I could see bags of green plastic army soldiers and shiny chrome toy handguns hanging out from the shelves. "Of course!" I considered to myself, toys should be near the end, by then the moms are worn out from their kids begging and crying and kicking. The chance of a conversion was much better. It's all in the timing.

A new line of weaponry was being exhibited and drew my upward, longing gaze. Plastic Civil War revolvers, designed after the Navy Colt looked perfect. And they shot vitamin-sized white plastic bullets. My mind leaped to the fun I could have with it. "Oh yes, I must have one," I whispered to myself.

Actually having a projectile fly from a handgun was a breakthrough for me. Within a week I was down to two of the original ten toy bullets. Lucky for me, I found that if I sharpened a #2 pencil down to an inch or less I could use it as a bullet. It couldn't fly as far as the plastic bullet, but did stick to cardboard and other soft, sometimes furry targets.

From this ordnance I graduated to loud, smoke making pop guns. My hunting buddy Larry also had a pop gun, and we would sneak into late summer corn fields and spook the growing numbers of red-winged blackbirds with a volley of pops. The flushing flock would whoosh upward with hundreds of birds that whirled and flew away.

To make smoke, Larry or I would cock the lever action pop gun and fire away rapidly. Soon curls of smoke would rise from the barrel and blow away when the gun was fired. We could blast ants off anthills and then, with a follow-up shot, blow the anthill away. Butterflies were puffed from green and lush milkweed, and later in the season, the milk-weed was exploded into hundreds of little para-chutists with a few burps from our brown steel pop guns. My toy eventually broke. The lever action lost the bolt holding it to the receiver and then I lost the lever. I put the pop gun away, planning on putting it back into service after finding the lever. It has been over fifty years now, and safe to say, it is the oldest proj-ect on my to-do list, although my wife may dis-agree.

My brothers both had hard shooting BB guns. The kind that could kill a pigeon roosting in a barn peak 40 feet up. They also shared a pellet gun, but loaned it to a friend and I never got my hands on it until I was a teenager. They eventually handed down their two pump action Daisy BB guns. By then only one worked, but it was fun to shoot. The end of the barrel unscrewed and out it came. The barrel and tube feed held about fifty copper-covered steel BBs. To load, you had to first compress the spring in the BB tube, and then place the BBs in one by one. A rather tedious process when having a rogue elephant charging out of the pasture at you.

Most BB guns I used had personalities of sorts. A gun would be missing a sight ramp, or always shoot left. This new rifle had no return spring behind the trigger, so that meant it could not be cocked after a shot until the trigger was pushed forward. I developed a double finger firing grip. The index finger squeezed the trigger, and my middle finger immediately returned it forward after discharge. My left hand held the plastic forestock and worked it back to cock. After some practice, I could lay down a field of fire at a respectable rate for the whole fifty rounds. It looked impressive on puddles and summer baked dirt.

The only way I could uncock my BB gun was to fire it, so when I was done for the day and going into the house, I always shot the last round as I stood on the back porch. An old bleach bottle with a small, wren-sized hole hanging from a pear tree thirty feet away was my main target from the porch. The BBs bounced off the bare white plastic, but a perfect shot went into the quarter-sized hole and rattled around. Over the years of my plinking away, I'm sure Mom often wondered why no birds nested in her recycling effort.

Sword Play

My twin sister almost blinded me in my right eye when we were six years old. She conked me with a stainless steel segment of vacuum cleaner tubing. We both had a section and were sword fighting. One end was designed to slide into the next for an airtight grip and was sharp enough to slice skin when at a high velocity.

After a morning of sitting still and watching classic movies with knights and sword battles my dear twin sister and I had a little extra energy and ran to Mom's Electrolux vacuum cleaner across the room. The attractive gray, red and chrome vacuum was always out and ready. Some sort of cleanup demanded its use almost daily, plus Mom hoped one of the kids just might actually use it.

To me it was a thing of beauty. It looked like a torpedo and sounded like a jet engine. It had no wheels, but pulled easily on chrome runners like a dog sled and had lots of parts that could be added or taken off. If I had been allowed to plug it in, I would have had it running most of the day. Amy and I would take turns riding it while the other pulled it around the carpeted living room and dining room oak floor.

We'd laugh and giggle when our hair was sucked up the hose. The tail of a slower house cat was sucked up one memorable day and from then on, just turning it on scared the kitty into a panic. It was a machine easy to love.

Mom was at her desk and clacking away with her new electric typewriter. It made the same sound with every keystroke, unlike her old manual typewriter that had a range of sounds from quick clicking runs to a solitary tunk made when she poked a number key with her index finger. She was working against a deadline and in a mental zone.

Two gleaming tubes that would make great shiny swords were clipped on the side of the cleaner and waiting. We took them and decided to go outside to the downslope of the yard and have a duel. We were re-creating the great swordplay on the movie castle steps.

We crossed swords to begin the challenge. I hauled back to unleash a sweeping slash. Amy, not hesitating from the start, did not pull back but chopped forward and caught me below my hairline over my right eye. End of fight. "Oh, Alex, you better show Mom," instructed Amy, "You're bleeding a lot!"

Crying, I went ahead of her into the

dining room. I was looking at Mom with my one good eye. The other was closed because blood was running down and over it. She was cradling her phone with her head on her shoulder and typing while smoking a cigarette. As soon as she saw me, I heard her say, "I have to go right now. I'll call you back," and had the phone hung up before she finished speaking. By the time she got to me, she had a cloth in her hand and started dabbing my forehead. She had seen enough headwounds to know that they bled like crazy. It was one of the reasons she always had a tissue or two up a sleeve.

It was a close call, but I didn't even need stitches. I never got a rematch with Amy. A new law had been decreed throughout the land, no more sword fighting. Her reign as champion swordsman would go unchallenged.

The vacuum cleaner was then stored in Mom and Dad's bedroom closet with the other household weapons.

I still made swords from scrap boards or wooden sticks, but went solo. When I fashioned a sword from a branch and felt it worthy, I would parry with an aluminum saucer sled hung from a ceiling crossbeam in the carriage house/garage. A round chrome shield with a colorful heraldic crest was fashioned for my left arm. Clothesline was knotted through drilled holes in the hubcap to make a grip and forearm brace. I was a knight of the realm of Cadillac. The wheel cover took a beating but was always a winner.

Dad used a sword to defend the house on a couple occasions. It's not that a sword was his first choice. He had a variety of other items within reach in his bedroom. Rifle, shotgun, pellet gun, handgun, knife, machete, tennis racket and golf club, to mention a few that were successfully used "off label."

The first time was a spring morning encounter with a scrappy ground hog. One of our smaller dogs had the woodchuck cornered against the farmhouse foundation. Pop used a vintage German artillery officers sword to dispatch the rodent and save the day.

The second time was in the waning moonlit darkness of early morning. A car had pulled in and backed out of the driveway and raced away three times that night. Dad was sure they had dropped off a thief and then came back to him. He called the county sheriff's dispatch office and went outside, grabbing a two iron from his golf bag on his way. The iron-armed man went to the front porch and waited in the darkness. In moments a car eased into the driveway, its lights off. My father left the porch and took up a defensive position behind a large arborvitae along the driveway. He could just see the outline of a car and a person coming around the front of it into the yard - right at the bush he was behind.

That was it for Dad. He raised the aluminum shafted "sword" and took aim at the intruder's head, but almost fell forward trying to stop. The target was wearing a deputy's hat with moonlight glinting off its badge.

"Howinell did you get here so fast?" Dad asked the officer. "Just lucky to be cruising by," said the unsuspecting and most lucky lawman.

Bullets and BBs

The first day I had my BB gun, I shot six hundred rounds with it. Our family was visiting our grandparents at their cottage on a bass filled lake and I shot at stuff all day, stopping only to eat and pee. It seemed normal to me at the time.

Tall trees blocked out most of the sunlight on the property and the north facing porch was always cool. Grandma and Grandpa had potted plants arranged around a number of tree trunks and had leftover broken stucco pots on a stump as a target for me. Over the afternoon I reduced them all to pieces and powder with my Daisy Spittin' image model 94 lever action carbine.

The gun was a dream come true to me. Since the age of ten I had admired the model in our town's appliance store. It was $12.95 and was the most money I had ever thought of. My allowance was twenty five cents a week, and was gone in days, so saving up to buy it was not likely.

On my twelfth birthday I knew as soon as I saw the wrapped package what it was. My dear sisters chipped in and bought me sixty cents worth of ammo, twelve packages of fifty

BBs each. Following this birthday on the farm, we loaded up the station wagon to go to the grandparents for another birthday celebration on the lake. All I needed was my BB gun and BBs. I could have left my swimming trunks home for all I cared about taking a dip on that day. The rifle and ammo were the finest assortment of gifts of all my preteen birthdays that I shared with my twin sister and mother.

When going afield, I'd carry my well-oiled BB gun, a tube of 250 BBs and my latest pocket knife. I had a hard time keeping a pocket knife. I lost a marble-handled Barlow within hours of getting it. In my pocket one afternoon and gone that night after running around the neighborhood. After a long spell of losing them, I developed a habit of keeping my eyes peeled and occasionally found other knives. I found an antler-handled Case hunting knife in the driveway of our farmhouse. It could have fallen from a plane for all I knew. I had never seen it before. It was the coolest thing I ever found in the driveway.

My twin sister Amy found a bloody bullet in the driveway. A man had pulled into the driveway in a light blue, early 1960s pickup, opened his door and stuck his head out. "Your daddy in the house?" asked the man. Amy and I were in the garage and told him yes. It wasn't unusual for a patient of Dad's to stop by to drop off some kind of payment or to just say hello.

We told the man Dad was home and went back to working on our bikes. The guy hobbled up the walk and knocked on the door of our house, calling for Doctor Weddon. He explained to Dad that he had been shot while backing out of a friend's driveway in his truck, the bullet going through the driver's door and hitting him. He drove straight to our farm.

Dad told the man he was calling the cops before helping him and closed the door in his face. My father, who had served in WWII as a combat medic, had quickly assessed the casualty as viable. He spoke to the county sheriff's office and then the hospital.

The gunshot victim grimaced and waited stoically on the porch until Dad returned. He told the wounded man he was going to live and sent him on his way to the hospital and waiting lawmen. Amy saw the bullet in the driveway gravel right after he left. She gave it to Dad who gave it to the sheriff's deputies that arrived later that afternoon. Our father shared a diagnostic technique with the note-taking deputies, "I knew he wasn't hurt that bad if he could stand on my porch for five minutes and not bleed to death," he offered.

My neighbors Larry and Ritchie and I had BB guns and shot at anything that came close to being a target. Dirt clods, cattails and milkweed pods all responded dramatically when drilled by a few BBs. Our guns were loaded with hundreds of rounds of the copper colored ammo. My rifle held a few over 40 and my friends could pour in 500 and shoot all week. They would shake their lever action rifles up and down to hear how many rounds were left.

Our BB guns shot hard enough to break a glass pop bottle after a few rounds. Another similarly aged and armed neighbor claimed his could kill a person but he'd have to shoot them in the eye. "Through your eye and right into your brain, yeah, yeah," declared Brian who only finished his serious sentences with a "yeah, yeah." It was a contraction of "yes, that's true, yes really." It was a common expression in our circle. We were so good at lying to each other that when speaking the truth, we had to issue a warning.

When the soggy early spring days warmed enough for the frogs to fill the nights with their croaking, it was time for a hunt. Larry and his brother Ritchie packed lunches for the all day excursion but soon ate the sand-wiches, keeping the wax paper to line the brown bags. Their mom could cook frog legs and her boys were out to fill their lunch bags with enough for a batch.

The three of us walked along miles of drainage ditch banks, mostly watching the green and black leopard frogs leap into the water and swim across the black muck bottom or downstream to hide under yellow blades of swampgrass.

We had learned to kill a frog so that it wouldn't leap into the water and get away. When shot between the eyes and just down the back a frog might stretch a leg, but died instantly without a reflex action.

It was a sunny and glorious day with a constant supply of frogs, jokes, shooting and tall tales. We worked both banks of a waterway at a time, picking up frogs another had shot. Before long, we had the two bags filled with slippery frogs warming up in the afternoon sun.

I don't know how the boys cleaned the sloppy mess of frogs, but they bragged that it was fine dining. "We had all we could eat, and that night, jumped up the stairs to our bedroom four steps at a time, yeah, yeah," they claimed.

Amy on left and Patrice, holding Horton.

Horton, the Greatest
of Horned Owls

A recent snowstorm with winds and freezing rain brought back the memory of one bird and his remarkable homing instinct. His name was Horton, a beautiful great horned owl that my older sister, my twin sister and I found one April day during a hike that took us far from our property line. The mature bird had a broken wing and was unafraid as we approached him near the edge of the woods we were leaving. We knew that injured wild animals should be left alone, or we could call a Conservation officer. Patrice, the elder of us at fourteen, picked him up with a gloved hand and that was it, the four of us trooped home.

His left wing was useless, but Horton could rise up and shrug out his shoulders to frightening proportions. We kept him in the basement where he would walk and climb about, and he was quite content to remain under the pool table when it was in use. He could still catch mice, and a squeal or a crashing from below our living room floor encouraged our rehabilitative hopes.

We didn't handle him much, but could easily approach him, as we often did to seek wise council or to collect a pellet. (To this day, I have trouble telling the difference.)

When the great horned owl hooted from his stone-walled basement, the booming notes resonated through the oaken floors and filled the house with a soul chilling sound that seemed to come from everywhere. Seven hoots to answer a relative roosting nearby.

As summer came to an end, it was decided to give Horton, whose fame had spread via newspapers and grapevine, to a neighbor who could take better care of him. The man wanted to use Horton as bait to hunt crows. The black marauders despise owls and will mob them whenever they can. The man would tether their most hated of all owls, the great horned owl, to a stump and have some good shooting.

The colors of fall turned to winter's black and white and blue. A storm crashed in from the east, lots of drifting snow and on the second day, freezing rain. That evening, Dad heard a scratching against the first floor bedroom window overlooking the porch. Thinking a limb had dropped from the weight of ice, he went to investigate. He was greeted by Horton, on his back, with his talons ready to tangle. The owl was wet, and in a most decidedly bad mood. The flightless bird had escaped who knows when and walked miles home. Here was a crippled bird, with so much against him, finding his way back to safety. We were awestruck by this display of never giving up, or, as my sister's gushed, eternal love.

After a few nights in the basement, we put Horton in the old chicken coop where he feasted on mice. The old bird never got over his bad mood. We'd leave corn to attract soon-to-be owl food, and could get near him, but he had changed. When he died a few months later, my sisters and I gave him a secret funeral under a blossoming pear tree.

The Last Tree Hut

Given enough scrap wood, farm boys in the 1960s could build about any kind of shelter seen in a National Geographic magazine. A favorite was making a summer retreat in the spreading limbs of a tree. Being in the shade, unseen and above most of the insects added to the attraction.

Construction plans for a new tree house started moments after a favorable tree was discovered. One summer hike took my neighbor Larry and me to a far away grove of oak trees. Located between two fields and along a drainage creek, the trees grew tall on the western slope of a natural ridge.

On the eastern edge, a tall, round white oak with outstretched limbs fifteen feet overhead offered a perfect location for a platform. Larry and I walked around the tree, stepping through a tangle of sharp raspberry canes and over fallen limbs and poison ivy. The tree was ideal for a tree house.

The big oak grew next to a field that was in corn that year and was a favorite for raccoons. Corn cobs from years before piled up around the base of the light barked trunk and hundreds more were beneath the outstretched limbs. Dark, seed-filled scat littered the area. The tree trunk was solid, no hollow for a 'coon family to occupy, but obviously the tree was a raccoon meeting hall of sorts. "What a great spot for a tree hut," declared Larry. "We'll see all kinds of deer and stuff from up there. It will be a perfect spot overnight when the moon's out, too!"

One of the best things about a tree hut was being able to look down on the rest of the world. Watching wild game was a great way to spend the afternoons on the farm, and Larry and I had stalked this very grove in the spring, sneaking up on a whitetail doe and her fawn. When she spotted us, only thirty feet away, she stiffened and stepped toward us. Larry shot up the nearest tree like a squirrel. I was left below. Looking up at his kicking boots and falling bark, I jumped to put the hickory between me and the charging doe. Nothing happened. Mom and baby ran away from all the movement and noise we made, but for a moment, both of us were trying to save our skin from an attacking deer. I wondered what Larry's reaction would be to a family of raccoons coming aboard our deck in the middle of the night.

"This is going to take a few boards more than usual," estimated Larry. For a thir-teen-year-old he had a good eye for building.

We decided to fashion a tree house big enough for sleeping bags and a trap door.

The limb closest to the ground was nine feet up. It would be a challenge just to get the wood up the tree. An abandoned tire chain was used as a ladder to gain access to the lowest limb. Then a scramble around the trunk and up to the construction site. Once Larry was straddling the foot thick limb, I would deliver boards and he would lay out the tree house deck.

We hiked back to the farm and to the pile of wood that used to be our old barn. The barn was demolished after the many accidents that followed a main floor cave-in. The old rotten barn had been stripped and then pulled down, but many parts of it lived on. Floor planks, beams and boards ended up as horse stalls, a stand-up bar, wall siding in a home's basement in town, dog houses and a variety of farm kid fashioned shelters we called huts.

Most of the sixteen foot siding boards had been salvaged by my older brothers Todd and Brad, but a few broken ones remained and we carried them across fences and fields the half mile to the tree.

The boards had a special provenance. The old barn had tried to kill most of us in the family. To name a few; it caved in on me, Amy was swinging on a rope over the hole made by the cave-in and plunged her thigh into a shard of floor board. She had to be pulled off that. Patrice had her head rammed into the ceiling by a jumpy quarter horse in the bottom level.

Larry and I had collected tools we felt worthy of being carried to the work site. We had an ancient pulley and lots of baler twine, a hammer and an old, dull, wood saw and a pocket of used and straightened nails. We hung the pulley above the two limbs and then threaded a twin strand of baler twine through the pulley and down. The thin twine could work its way off the pulley and wedge between the round wood spindle and iron frame, so we had to be careful to hoist directly in line beneath the tackle.

The pine barn boards were over a foot wide and had shrunken to about 3/4 of an inch thick over the eighty or so years of exposure to Michigan weather. We were able to transport about twenty boards of three to nine foot lengths over a couple of weeks. Larry and I carried two at a time and stopped frequently to let the blood back into our fingers. To pass the time, we talked of other historic efforts in construction. We started with the slaves building the pyramids.

"I'll bet they didn't have mosquitoes pestering them," said Larry during a break.

"Yeah, I'm sure they didn't, but if you pass out from exhaustion, I won't use your guts to grease the way, either," I countered.

Our trips from pile to tree gave us the chance to be soldiers climbing the Alps with Hannibal and his elephants, Lewis and Clark carrying boats over the plains of the West, turn of the century explorers going to the North Pole with barn wood toboggans pulled by Huskies, "Hey, there are no trees at the North Pole!" observed Larry, "I know that, we are going to make a raft and float home on it," I offered. We'll head for home in the summer when the ice is melted, of course," I guessed.

The "V" shaped deck was level enough to the naked eye, but we put up a board railing inches above the board's edges just to be safe. Rolling off was often the subject of the last exchange when we settled in for a night in a tree hut.

As it turned out, we only spent a couple moonlit nights in the old oak. Most of the time the place was used to spend the afternoons watching game or stretched out, looking up at a sparkling summer sun through the leaves. It was the last tree hut we built.

We had slept in trees before. During one campout earlier that summer, we were walking back along a moonlit lane after a late foray into town. As we approached a rattling grove of poplar trees, we challenged each other to climb up one and spend the rest of the night in it.

Falling asleep after wedging yourself between treetrunk and limb took some concentration. Trying to overcome the creeping paralysis in the extremities was another challenge. The sensation of a numb leg doesn't add much to a sense of safety, either. Try as I might, I could only lapse off for a minute or two before a desperate need to adjust my contorted body overcame me. Larry fell asleep, twitched, and jerked his head up. We didn't sleep much that night, but did come up with some ideas for the next overnighter. A Velcro shirt and pants would make a dandy combo to attach to a tree. An inflatable suit to make a tight wedge, a sleeping back hung like an Oriole's nest, like those used by mountain climbers. Hanging a hammock between spreading limbs thirty feet up was a good idea we never tried.

As soon as the morning sun peeked over the eastern horizon we dismounted. Our blood starved limbs and sleep deprivation caused us to walk to our campsite bent like old ladies pushing shopping carts.

As we approached the picnic table, we saw that the hot dogs, buns and now stale potato chips had been left out. This was common for us. As the night waned, so did our sense of food safety. Cleaning up before falling asleep didn't become an option until after the campout when we lost all our food to raccoons or aliens. We still debate which creature launched that invasion.

WINTER

Christmas Break

The season went into high gear the moment my sisters and I leapt from our school bus and galloped up our driveway, shouting "See you next year!" to our classmates and bus driver on the day Christmas vacation started.

The school day had crawled along, our teachers relenting and allowing the students a half day of fun after we cleaned out our desks in preparation for our return to start another semester and fresh new year.

My fourth grade teacher made sure that when cleaning my desk, I scraped the housefly encased in dried glue from my desktop. "It was the first thing your mother saw at last night's PTA meeting," she admonished.

Days before, our class had made Christmas tree decorations and long chains made of red and green construction paper links using almost sharp scissors and glue made from, according to my dear twin sister Amy, horses' hooves. The glue label said "non-toxic" and that meant it wouldn't kill us to eat it or get it in our hair. Most of us were content to apply the bitter tasting glue to our fingers, let it dry and then peel off the fake skin.

For a common housefly, it was toxic, but not immediately. For reasons unknown, my desk had a fair share of air traffic over it and occasionally the flies would land to rest before continuing their search for unprotected lunches. I had dripped a postage stamp sized amount of glue on my desk and waited, completely distracted from the Spanish lesson being televised on the TV in the room.

A large bluebottle fly circled and landed directly onto my sticky glue. It struggled to free itself to no avail. The wings buzzed for two or three seconds and stopped, as if to recharge. Then another buzz. This drew the attention of my nearby classmates.

"Cut it in half with the scissors," whispered Jeff.

"Pull its wings off," came another thoughtful suggestion.

"Smash it into a bloody goo," came another tempting whisper from the girl behind me.

A fly of this size was a real trophy and after reading about dinosaurs in tar pits and dragonflies trapped in pine sap, I decided to make my own fly amber. I held the glue bottle upside down above the now exhausted insect. A dollop of golden glue landed and the process began. By the end of the day it had dried clear and was most impressive to my friends. But on this day before Christmas break, my archeological efforts went unappreciated by my teacher.

She strolled between students, her eyes scouring desk surfaces for unacceptable accessories or defacement. She paused briefly at my desk, raised an eyebrow and deftly swept my artifact into her brown metal wastebasket, consigning my newest treasure to the dust heap of history to await a future generation of investigators to unearth it and marvel.

I didn't say anything about my array of chewing gum stalactites under my tilt-up desk top as she moved on, my friends filling her wastebasket with the common debris of education and flotsam from the lives of nine-year-olds.

Once the room met with the sanitary approval of the teacher, we were allowed a longer than usual lunch recess as the gym/lunch room was prepared for the afternoon Christmas plays.

And now we were free. The school bus drove on with a number of eager kids still on board and captive, but we were free! Our delight was reflected in the joyous yapping of our pack of farm dogs that would meet us in the driveway and escort us to the back door of our farmhouse.

119

One amazing Christmas years later, a large cardboard box, set on its narrow edge, occupied most of our parlor next to the home-grown Christmas tree. It was bigger than the piano and caused a great deal of discussion among my siblings.

"I don't see any air holes for a pony," guessed Amy. "It's my helicopter!" said Brad wishfully. "I want the box for a deer blind," claimed oldest brother Todd. Whatever it was, we couldn't wait until Christmas day to open the monster. It took up almost the whole room and we needed the space for more presents.

Mom and Dad held a private, low voiced conference in the kitchen. "Kids, we received a special note from the North Pole, giving us permission to open it now, instead of waiting." Almost before they had finished giving us the glorious news we were attacking the box to open it. Inside was a full sized pool table, and we danced around it in pure joy.

"Where are we going to put it?" we asked. "Well, there's room in the basement, if we move the ping-pong table. We called the store and they are sending some men to put it up today," Mom said with a smile.

The two men labored mightily to slide, tip and push the heavy slate table around the basement door and onto the steps. There just wasn't enough clearance. It wasn't going down that way. The verdict saddened us.

One of the men noticed that directly over the basement steps was the stairway to the attic. "If we pull the attic steps out, there should be plenty of room," he judged.

A chance to disassemble anything was all that older brothers Todd and Brad needed to hear and the two sprang into action. In moments the treads and risers of the steps were pried and knocked free. The dust was still settling as the table was lowered into the gaping hole that once was the stairway to the farm-hand's room in the attic.

Soon the sharp crack of pool balls was heard along with Christmas carols and melodies throughout the house. The balls made a merry sound as they rolled along the metal rails below the tabletop after plunking into a pocket.

By nightfall, word of "Weddon's Pool Hole" had spread to our neighbors. A steady stream of challengers piled coats and boots and gloves by the basement door and joined in the fun.

As Christmas Eve approached, Mom evaluated the carnage of broken and split wood that used to be the attic steps with a look of concern. It seems that some of Santa's stash was up there, and unless his reindeer could fly up and get them, things could get testy Christmas morning. She approached Patrice, the older and more discreet sister, with a request. "Oh Mom, we all know," she admitted. "A little elf told me about the presents last week. This morning, that little elf turned into a monkey and climbed up there and moved them to the bathroom closet. But now," she objected, "all the tags say 'To Alex, from Santa.'"

Winter Effects

As an elementary school-aged kid, it was always difficult for me to stay inside during Christmas break. I would guess it is the same for today's preteens. For me it was a way to get out and explore the effect of winter on our farm.

The cold weather brought on changes inside as well. Dry winter winds, howling down from Canada, could move the heavy living room curtains of our 1890s farmhouse. The kitchen was the warmest place in the house when the stove and oven were going. A heat duct spilled hot air from the toe kick under the sink, heating the surrounding vinyl floor. It felt good under our socked feet.

The thermostat that controlled the fuel oil burning furnace was located at eye level on the wall near Mom and Dad's bedroom and was under their authority. I don't remember ever touching it, but did look at it often. So did Dad. He would take a reading whenever the furnace kicked on.

Not to say it was cold on the main floor of the house, but suffice it to reason that during the winter season, no virus or bacterium exposed to this environment could survive.

"Good preventive medicine," he would declare and spin the thermostat, countering Mom's turning it up to get enough heat in the back-room to dry the pile of snow-soaked coats, gloves and hats.

There was a strategy for keeping warm when wearing only tee shirts and pajama bottoms. When the furnace whomped and fired up, we'd plop down by a heat register and hold open our shirts, inflating them with delicious warmth.

Getting heat upstairs was a test of wills. My older and craftier brother Todd once engaged Mom and Dad in a conversation about Jules Verne's novel *Around the World in 80 Days*, and paused after describing the hot air balloon rising far into the freezing atmosphere. "It was so cold their eyeballs almost froze in their sockets," he described to the now impressed and attentive parents. "And that's what will happen to me upstairs in my bedroom unless the heat gets turned up." Dad bumped the heat up a degree just for his originality.

Christmas break was more fun with snow to play in. Some years we had plenty of snow, others we had none or freezing rain. In Michigan winters, temperatures can easily plunge below freezing in an afternoon.

One shift caused havoc on roads after a high school basketball game. We had driven to Chelsea to watch older brother Brad play in a Christmas tournament. By the time we left the game, the temperature had dropped so that the pelting rain was freezing onto everything it hit. The next day I skated down the road to my neighbor's house. The half-mile sortie included a hill, and I remember thinking how funny it was to skate on ice, uphill.

Larry and I soon skated down that hill with expectations of Olympic speeds, but there were unavoidable blots of dry pavement that had a considerable negative effect on our velocity.

Walking on the lake's first ice always raised the same mental questions. How thick is it? Will it hold? Is it rotten? How deep is it here?

The dogs could sense our concerns. After a few minutes and walking back on our tracks, Larry and I would gain confidence. Before long the pack was running around or sliding with us.

You can't trust creek ice, ever. I never liked walking on a frozen creek when hunting or hiking. It didn't matter how cold the winter had been, I always trudged along the creek bank and for good reason.

One high school winter break, Todd and neighbors Denny and Linda were poking along on the ice of the creek that ran along and then under the road by their house. They were in a spot that had some history.

That length of ditch almost claimed Linda one summer. The three of them and Brad were kicking up frogs and throwing rocks and sticks and making dares when Linda fell into a deep, slower part of the creek. She quickly got up, but by then bloodsuckers had glommed onto her. The dark brown, inch long, glistening ribbons turned and twisted in the summer sun. Some curled; others extended and moved across the exposed skin of her back. When she clawed her fingers through her hair and came away with a writhing, slug-like critter, she vaulted into a legendary fit of hysterics. Her near delirious, white-out fear was augmented by the well-intentioned efforts of Todd.

The lad was helping her run across a field to her house, as she was having some motor skill difficulties. Linda's escalating frenzy was due in part to my brother's counting out loud as he plucked away. Her fear crazed zigzagging and falling into a weeping ball a few times were challenges for Todd, but he persisted, and stayed with her, announcing the growing 'sucker tally all the way to the backdoor.

The final number is still in dispute, but somewhere north of twenty is well accepted.

This winter day, Todd and Linda were ahead of Denny, who was making his own tracks instead of following along in theirs. Sure enough, he fell into the shallow, muckbottomed creek. The shocking cold of the water sucked a startled yell back into his lungs and he went under, feet first.

Denny rolled under the ice, his hands and feet trying to keep him stable. He knew if he could get his feet under him and stand up, the ice would give way and he could get out. Linda was looking down at her feet as she walked along a stretch of clear ice. It was timing only a sister could possess.

"Todd, look at that seal!" she shouted, astonished as Denny went under her, twisting in the current.

"That's not a seal," Todd yelled. "It's Denny."

Todd jumped to the creekbank where Denny surfaced. The gurgling current over a shallow run had not frozen. He grabbed Denny by his belt and helped him out.

"Hey Denny, did you see a seal when you were swimming around?" joked Todd as the three ran up a familiar path to the waiting warmth of their homes.

Thin Ice

Uneven winter weather can make for dangerous ice. A few winters ago I was hiking along a shoreline and punched through the ice in over my boots. The knee high soaking was a shock, and minutes later, when I was drying my boots and socks near a campfire, I thought of the winter one of our dogs fell into the creek that cuts across the farm.

It was a Saturday in March many years ago. I could hear barking and it sounded different. I recognized the "Barp Barp Barp" of Bozo, a liver and white springer spaniel that had adopted us years earlier when the family was driving around in our stationwagon looking for one of Dad's truant Brittanys. We never found Max, but did come home with Bozo. He was a loyal sidekick to us all and now something wasn't right. I went back inside and watched an episode of *Fury* on the television.

Later that afternoon, I was outside with my sisters and could hear Bozo still barking. Three barks, pause, then three more. He was in distress. We went to investigate and moved quickly across the big pasture to the creek just across the far pasture fence. We got close enough to see the snow white ribbon of the creek open into a black swirl of water with Bozo in the middle, hanging onto the icy ledge on the upstream side. He would bark three times as the current stretched him, stop and pull himself up, and then bark three more times as the current again pulled him. The ice cold waterline was midway up his chest. He had been in the water for at least four hours. How much longer could he hang on? We couldn't get close to the bank, the ice was rotten and dangerous. We stood helpless and looked on and listened to Bozo.

We had been there only a few minutes when my oldest brother, Todd, arrived with a board from the old barn, a sixteen footer, over a foot wide and an inch thick. He ran a trap line along the creek and had the gear to get into the water if he had to. Todd made it to the creekbank upstream, pushed the board across the snow and under Bozo's slashing front paws. The dog pulled himself out and made for Todd, stopping to shake at our brother's feet as thanks for saving his life. It was a real live rescue.

Todd made me and my sisters carry the board back to the barn while he and the victim made their way back to the warm kitchen.

Bozo seemed to be just fine. He picked up a favorite toy, a heavy bowling pin, and walked away with it. The lopsided weight twisting his head to and fro with each step.

Winter Rat Invasion

Single digit cold weather is rough on outdoor animals. Warm blooded critters seek out warmer environs, as it was years ago in our farmhouse.

Cold and vermin constantly probed our walls, windows and doors. This assault was somewhat slowed by the bales of straw we put up against the stone foundation, but more often than not, the bales became a snug harbor for mice, rabbits, opossum and the occasional skunk.

One particularly cold winter had below zero temperatures for days on end. For extra warmth going out to do my chores, I would pull plastic bread bags over my socks when putting on my boots. In the evening, frozen gloves stood like reaching hands over the heat registers on the dining room floor.

Spit freezing cold like this would cause grain fed Norway rats to migrate from under the oat bin in our barn into our house. My sisters, brothers and I could hear them at night as we lay in our beds under extra quilts. The midnight monsters would scurry up and down within the wall partitions. Banging on the walls would briefly stop them. When we would get snug and start to drift off to sleep, they would start up again.

The big rats were fearless. We kept our 40 pound bag of dog food on the landing at the top of the basement stairs. The rats would tear into it and feed and were loath to be dislodged by a skinny fifteen-year-old who was assigned to feed the dogs everyday. My skin would crawl when I could hear them fighting. I would rattle the basement door before opening it, hoping to scare them away. We put out rat traps as big as the family Bible on the steps below and around the dogfood bag. The traps were scary even to set. We used dog food for bait, of course. After catching three or four, they wised up and avoided them.

At night, when the winter winds would rip from the north, making our rooftop TV antennae hum, I would dream of an undulating carpet of rats sweeping from the barn to the house and pouring in.

Our family of seven would gather in the living room on Sunday nights to watch TV. We enjoyed *Walt Disney Presents*, then *Car Fifty-Four Where Are You* and at nine o'clock, *Bonanza*.

One night, before the start of *Bonanza*, Dad got up from his recliner with a shoe in his hand, walked between the pocket doors separating the living room from the dining room and suddenly stooped over and slammed the

131

shoe down, killing a rat that none of us had even seen. We were wide eyed after that, and all of us on the davenport jerked our feet off the floor to underneath a shared afghan.

A few days later, my twin sister Amy was in the bathroom and called out to me in a quiet voice, "Alex, come in here, a rat is staring at me!" When I opened the door, there sat Amy, looking back at a rat the size of a cat, perched on the edge of the bathtub, maybe a yardstick away from her face. Now, any wild animal that isn't afraid of people is most likely sick and dangerous. And any wild animal that is cornered is dangerous. Both conditions applied to this rat. Amy sat motionless, knowing full well not to move. The rat sat up and turned to look at me. I was two steps into the bathroom and drove a booted foot into him, driving him across the tub and into the wall of the shower enclosure. The beast fell into the ceramic tub, all four paws futilely scratching to gain purchase. I brought down my boot heel onto his head and heard a satisfying crunch. Blood streaked toward the tub drain, the rough scaled tail curled and was still. The shower scene in *Psycho* had nothing on this frightful sight.

Amy finished her paperwork, calmly thanked me, washed her hands and left, passing

Dad. He came in, surveyed the scene of the rescue and uttered an oath or two, dropped the animal into a paper grocery sack, turned on the shower and rinsed the tub.

From then on, I always wore shoes when using the bathroom. Come to think of it, everyone else did too.

The details of the close calls in this book have been refined over many tellings during family meals or holiday gatherings. A few made it to print in newspapers, magazines, family Christmas letters, police reports and school board minutes prior to my chronicling them.

I close this collection with a 1988 Christmas time letter to my brothers and sisters.

Doc's Holiday

Dear Siblings,

Having just received the news over the wire from Miss Willah, I felt that the rest of the clan should know of the latest gunplay at the homestead.

Being the holiday season and that some of us may journey back home, this account should stand as more of an advisement than anything else.

As you know, Doc has been packing bad medicine for the bloodthirsty varmints that perpetrated that daring midnight raid in our home this summer. They drew first blood and made good their escape, not to mention our father's indignity of having needles poked into him to stave off hydrophobia.

Anyhow, it seems that Ma heard some kind of ruckus coming from the necessary room. Well, that's not all that unusual, except that she was sure no one was in there. The noises lacked the usual ceramic resonance.

Thus alerted, she went for Pa, who was hunkered down in his favorite chair, checking his eyelids for cracks. "I heard something scratching around in the bathroom linen closet," she whispered. "Could be your furry friend."

In less time than it takes to tell, Doc was on his feet and heading for his hardware. Figuring to settle the rodent feud account in full, he filled his hand with a golf club, and then his eyes took on a flinty stare. Looking at his reflection in the mirror over his bureau, he replaced the vintage two iron.

What he did next was due, in part, to a couple of things. One of which was the fact that the game pole rope in the barn was a bit light, this being the time of the year when it usually swings to the contrary.

Or maybe it was an itchy trigger finger. His model 12 hadn't fired since bird season. Going too long between successful hunts can change a man.

In any case, Doc set the table. He'd been biding his time and now could make his move to settle things.

Exercising his penchant for fair chase, his fist went past the twelve gauge and clenched around the double barrel twenty. With a practiced move that he could do in the dark, he broke it open and chambered a brace of low brass #9 shells.

Turning on his heels, he snapped the piece closed and held it at the ready, thumb on the safety.

Ma went into the bathroom first, hoping to flush the trespasser out. After taking two steps in she heard something and froze, her eyes fixed. Pa moved in on Ma's left flank. Something was behind the closet doors, waiting. He cocked his head to one side, trying to determine which closet door to rush.

Miss Willah, now looking over Doc's shoulder, allowed that the interloper certainly picked the right spot for sanctuary. Holing up in a closet filled with Christmas gifts would certainly put a premium on shot placement.

He grunted an acknowledgement. Gifts or not, Doc's mind was set. When the smoke cleared, it wouldn't be his carcass going over the bank to the garbage heap.

A muted rustle said left closet door. As quick as a Diamondback, Doc played his hand. The door flew open. He now had a bead drawn between the eyes of the problem.

Their eyes met, an instant later hot lead filled the air and it was over.

Her ears ringing, Ma stooped over and picked up the larger of the body parts lying on the floor. She held it up to Pa.

Not often seen in these parts, he still recognized what was left of a flying squirrel. He figured it probably went 6, maybe 7 ounces, live weight.

Puny in comparison to that woodchuck that had him cornered a few years back. He'd made quick work of it with nothing more than a World War One vintage saber. And he mused, not quite as challenging as taking on a Sheriff's deputy with a two iron in the driveway, Nevertheless, the homestead was now secure.

Sure, maybe a few presents had to be re-wrapped, but if they acted quickly, they could wipe off the stains. Nothing a little hard work couldn't fix. A small price to pay for a safe Christmas.

With a sense of relief, Ma squeezed Pa's hand. Life was good.

Well, that about does it. Just be advised that when you get your gift, it may have some extra ventilation. And the wrapping paper may have some unusual coloring, too.

Hopefully, by the time you recycle it for use again next year, the reds and greens will look natural.

One more item to note. True to form, Mom salvaged what she could and you can now see the tail of that squirrel swinging from the clothesline. With a little luck, it won't be seen by eight gun-shy reindeer.

Merry Christmas!
#3 son

---the end--
Close Calls on the Farm: *Survival of the Funniest*

———————————

More Close Calls available!

Alex's second in the series is
Close Calls on the Farm: *Second Chances*
and third is
Close Calls on the Farm: *Off to School*
> **www.closecallsonthefarm.com** to order

From the Table of Contents:

From the Table of Contents - (Tx 2 Judy Lee)

www.CloseCallsOnTheFarm.com
for ordering information.
